# CHARACTERS
# AND
# DOCTRINES

**Nadab to Boaz**
E. M. BLAIKLOCK, M.A., D.Litt.

**The Character of God**
J. STAFFORD WRIGHT, M.A.

WILLIAM B. EERDMANS PUBLISHING COMPANY
GRAND RAPIDS, MICHIGAN

SCRIPTURE UNION IN NORTH AMERICA

U. S. A.:  38 Garrett Road, Upper Darby,
           Pennsylvania 19082
Canada:    5 Rowanwood Avenue, Toronto 5,
           Ontario

Printed in the United States of America.

Each volume of Bible Characters and Doctrines is divided into the right number of sections to make daily use possible, though dates are not attached to the sections because of the books' continuing use as a complete set of character studies and doctrinal expositions. The study for each day is clearly numbered and the Bible passage to be read is placed alongside it.

Sections presenting the characters and doctrines alternate throughout each book, providing balance and variety in the selected subjects. At the end of each section there is a selection of questions and themes for further study related to the material covered in the preceding readings.

Each volume will provide material for one quarter's use, with between 91 and 96 sections. Where it is suggested that two sections should be read together in order to fit the three-month period, they are marked with an asterisk.

The scheme will be completed in four years. Professor E. M. Blaiklock, who writes all the character studies, will work progressively through the Old and New Testament records. Writers of the doctrinal sections contribute to a pattern of studies drawn up by the Rev. Geoffrey Grogan, Principal of the Bible Training Institute, Glasgow, in his capacity as Co-ordinating Editor. A chart overleaf indicates how the doctrinal sections are planned.

In this series biblical quotations are normally taken from the RSV unless otherwise identified. Occasionally Professor Blaiklock provides his own translation of the biblical text.

## DOCTRINAL STUDY SCHEME

|  | Year 1 | Year 2 | Year 3 | Year 4 |
|---|---|---|---|---|
| First Quarter | The God who Speaks | Man and Sin | The Work of Christ | The Kingdom and the Church |
| Second Quarter | God in His World | Law and Grace | Righteousness in Christ | The Mission of the Church |
| Third Quarter | The Character of God | The Life of Christ | Life in Christ | The Church's Ministry and Ordinances |
| Fourth Quarter | The Holy Trinity | The Person of Christ | The Holy Spirit | The Last Things |

# DOCTRINAL STUDIES

## THE CHARACTER OF GOD

Study

### A Personal God

1  The Great Name                Exodus 3.1–15
2  God is not Less than Man      Psalm 94
3  Father and Child              Hosea 11.1–9

### A Holy and Righteous God
### (a) Disclosed in Old Testament History

13  The Hand of God in
      Destruction and Renewal   Genesis 6.9—7.4; 8.13-22
14  God Sees a Spark of
      Righteousness             Genesis 19.1–29
15  God's Character as His
      Will for Man              Exodus 20.1–20
16  Principle of Obedience to
      God                       1 Samuel 15
17  God and the Family          2 Samuel 12.1–25
18  Unholy History              2 Kings 17.1–28
19  Dangerous Future            1 Kings 8.22–53
20  God Gives no Blank Cheque   1 Kings 8.54—9.9
21  History as His Story        Ezra 9

### (b) Declared in Psalm and Prophecy

30  Vindication by the Righteous
      God                       Psalm 7
31  Call to the Nations         Psalm 99
32  The Holy One of Israel      Isaiah 6
33  Substitutes for God-likeness Isaiah 1
34  Substitutes for God's Truth  Jeremiah 7
35  Ruin that God will not
      Prevent                   Ezekiel 7
36  God's Will and the Common
      Conscience                Amos 1.1—2.3
37  Sin Against God's Revealed
      Truth                     Amos 2.4–16

Study

## (c) Displayed in Gospel and Epistle

45 God's Judgement, Present
    and Future      Matthew 3
46 God's Work from Within      Luke 11.37–53
47 The Rejection of God in
    Christ      Luke 20.1–18
48 Open to God and Man      Acts 5.1–16
49 A Lost Eternity      2 Thessalonians 1
50 Presuming on God      Hebrews 10.26–39
51 The Life of God-likeness      1 Peter 1.13–25

# A Merciful and Compassionate God
## (a) Revealed in History and Psalm

60 The Line of Divine Promise      Genesis 15
61 A Promise and a Prayer      Genesis 18
62 Friend with Friend      Exodus 33, 34
63 Covenant Love      Deuteronomy 7.6–26
64 God's Ways      1 Samuel 1.1—2.10
65 The Open Way      Psalm 27
66 Companion by the Way      Psalm 34
67 Pilgrim's Progress      Psalm 107

## (b) Proclaimed in Prophecy

77 Announcement of the
    Gospel      Isaiah 55
78 God in the Darkness      Lamentations 3
79 God the Good Shepherd      Ezekiel 34
80 Mercy for the Prophet      Jonah 1, 2
81 God's Mercy for Nineveh      Jonah 3, 4

## (c) Exhibited in Christ

87 Merciful as God      Matthew 11.25—12.21
88 To be like God      Luke 6.17–38
89 God calls the Gentiles      Acts 10
90 The Glory of being a
    Christian      Ephesians 1
91 The Way into God      Ephesians 2
92 Full Members in Christ      Ephesians 3
93 God is Totally Love      1 John 4.7–21

# CHARACTER STUDIES

## NADAB TO BOAZ

Study
| | | |
|---|---|---|
| 4 | Nadab and Abihu | Leviticus 10.1–11 |
| 5 | Caleb | Numbers 13, 14; Deuteronomy 1; Joshua 14.6–15 |
| 6 | Korah | Numbers 16 |
| 7 | Balaam | Numbers 22.1–31 |
| 8 | Balaam's Conscience | Numbers 22.32–41 |
| 9 | Balaam the Prophet | Numbers 23.1–26 |
| 10 | Balak | Numbers 23.27–30 |
| 11 | Balaam Again | Numbers 24 |
| 12 | Balaam's Baseness | Numbers 25 |
| 22 | Joshua Son of Nun | Exodus 17.13, 14; 24.13; 32.17, 18; 33.7–11 |
| 23 | Joshua Takes Over | Deuteronomy 3.21–29; 34.1–12; Joshua 1 |
| 24 | Joshua's Encouragement | Deuteronomy 31.7, 8, 22, 23; 1 Corinthians 16.13 |
| 25 | Nun | Deuteronomy 4.9, 10; 6.7, 20–24; 11.18–21; 32.46 |
| 26 | Rahab | Joshua 2.1–24; 6.17, 22–25; Hebrews 11.31; James 2.25 |
| 27 | The New Joshua | Joshua 3, 4 |
| 28 | King of Jericho | Joshua 5, 6 |
| 29 | Achan | Joshua 7; 1 Chronicles 2.7 |
| 38 | Joshua Relives the Past | Joshua 8 |
| 39 | Adonizedek | Joshua 10 |
| 40 | Joshua's Success | Joshua 11 |
| 41 | Caleb | Joshua 14 |
| 42 | Phinehas | Joshua 22 |
| 43 | Joshua's Charge | Joshua 23.1—24.28 |
| 44 | Joshua's Passing | Joshua 24.29–33; Judges 2.1–10 |

7

Study

| | | |
|---|---|---|
| 52 | The Judges | Judges 1–3 |
| 53 | Deborah and Barak | Judges 4, 5 |
| 54 | Deborah's Song | Judges 5 |
| 55 | Gideon | Judges 6.1–27 |
| 56 | Joash | Judges 6.28–32 |
| 57 | Gideon's Testing | Judges 6.33—7.7 |
| 58 | Gideon's Victory | Judges 7.8–8.21 |
| 59 | Gideon at Peace | Judges 8.22–28 |
| | | |
| 68 | Abimelech | Judges 8.29—9.57 |
| 69 | Jephthah | Judges 11 |
| 70 | Jephthah's End | Judges 12 |
| 71 | Samson's Parents | Judges 13 |
| 72 | Young Samson | Judges 14 |
| 73 | Samson's Folly | Judges 15 |
| 74 | Samson's Failure | 2 Corinthians 6 |
| 75 | Delilah | Judges 16.1-22 |
| 76 | Samson's End | Judges 16.23-31 |
| | | |
| 82 | Micah | Judges 17 |
| 83 | Moses' Descendant | Judges 18 |
| 84 | Naomi | Ruth 1 |
| 85 | Ruth | Ruth 1.15—2.23 |
| 86 | Boaz | Ruth 3, 4 |

# THE CHARACTER OF GOD

INTRODUCTION

In studying the character of God we must be careful not to fall into these extremes: i. 'God cannot be known, but can only be experienced.' Yet He has told us about Himself in Scripture, and we must use our God-given intelligence to understand what He has said. ii. 'God can be studied and analysed as a scientist studies a beetle.' Although God has revealed Himself, He cannot be fully comprehended by finite creatures. iii. 'God cannot be personal in any meaningful sense.' God is not A person limited by a body, but we, who are persons, find revealed in Him those qualities that we call personal.

# THE CHARACTER OF GOD

## A Personal God

### 1 : The Great Name

#### Exodus 3.1–15

The revelation of God as 'I AM' (14) shows Him as the uncreated source of all existence. 'I AM' is the 1st person singular of the word which in the 3rd person becomes the Name Jehovah, Yahweh, or LORD (15), meaning HE IS. This is always printed in capitals in the RSV in the hundreds of places where it occurs. It was not an entirely new Name, but had not previously been the Name of Covenant relationship (Exod. 6.2, 3). This Name at once lifts God out of the realm of idols, although the four Hebrew letters (the Tetragrammaton) have often been used as a magical charm.

The content of the Name can form a helpful meditation, so long as it does not lead to a conception of impersonal Being. The setting here is important, since the I AM shows Himself (not Itself) to be personally concerned about His people (7), and to be taking deliberate steps to deliver them (8).

Yet v. 10 gives a fundamental point about God's working. As personal, He uses persons like Moses to do His will (10), in accordance with His original purpose of creating man to rule the world as His representative (Gen. 1.26–28). Moses will find strength in God's presence with him (12, cf. Matt. 28.19, 20). We note the margin of v. 14. The Name I AM is in the uncompleted tense in Hebrew, so that it includes the future. We never have to say, 'God *was*' or 'God is dead'.

The vision of the burning bush confirmed this presentness.

Moses knew that God had communicated with the patriarchs in sensory form. Sometimes this was called an appearance of THE angel of the Lord, although this angel speaks as God (e.g. Gen. 16.7–13). So here the flame hides, while the voice reveals, the angel of the Lord (2), who is the Lord Himself (4). It is likely that this angel of the Lord is the Second Person of the Trinity in a pre-incarnation appearance.

*Meditate on the I AM in John* **8.58**.

## 2 : God is not Less than Man

### Psalm 94

The key verses here are vs. 7–9. We cannot suppose that man is aware of all the happenings in the world, while God is blind and deaf to them. Yet the psalmist faces a problem that is still with us. Criminals of all grades act on the assumption either that there is no God, or that they can get away with whatever they want to do, and God will not interfere with them (3–7).

One of the lessons that keeps emerging in these studies is that the personal God normally works as Person with person. Having created man to be His representative in managing the world (Gen. 1.26–28), He looks for man to turn to Him for guidance and strength. The heart of the Fall was man's decision to be self-governing instead of God-centred (Gen. 3.5). And, since man is not a puppet for God to manipulate, God does not normally force him to go His way, but uses the means by which person influences person.

Thus the psalmist begins by crying out for God's violent intervention (1–3), then realizes that God is even more aware of man's distress than he is himself (9–11), and so turns to God to teach and use him as a person. Sufferings that come through human sin may be transmuted through sharing them with other persons, and above all with the personal God (12–15).

God Himself will stir us up to resist wrongdoing (16). Without the assurance of God's present inner help (17–19), and His declared horror of evil (20), we might well be hesitant. Even though we make slow progress now, we can bear witness to God's vindication of His people (14, 15), and we know

11

that the day will come when God will actively intervene to judge the world and put out all that spoils His creation (23, cf. Mal. 3.16—4.3).

*From a different angle, think of vs. 9–11 when you watch a TV programme, or read a book, on the body and brain of man. Could everything emerge without a personal Creator?*


# 3 : Father and Child

## Hosea 11.1–9

This is one of the rare passages in the Old Testament where God speaks of Himself as Father, an intensely personal description. Earlier in Hosea He is the husband with the unfaithful wife (ch. 2). Now he has the grief that even Christian parents sometimes know. One cannot press every detail in the analogy, since God did not beget the nation. Hence we start with the concept of God's personal love, calling, and family acceptance of His people, corresponding to our own calling and adoption in Christ (e.g. Gal. 4.4–7).

The picture goes back to the earliest days—the Father's acceptance of the baby as His own (1), picking him up in His arms (3), teaching him to walk with leather reins to keep him from falling (3, 4), and removing any constrictions that would hinder easy feeding (4; an emendation gives an easier sense; 'I had lifted them like a little child to my cheek', NEB and Jer. Bible). The father's love was spurned, and the child ran off like the Prodigal Son (Luke 15.13).

The application is that the personal God was exchanged by Israel for dead idols (2, cf. 2.5). The only satisfactory way that Person could now deal with persons was to let them go to the far country, as the father let the prodigal go. Israel will repeat the Egyptian bondage in Assyria (5), whose king took them into captivity in 721 B.C. We shall read of this later in 2 Kings 17.1–28.

The Father still loves His child and does not let him be destroyed (8; for Admah and Zeboiim see Gen. 14.2; Deut. 29.23). He is not a bitter man who rejects him (9). But, as with the Southern Kingdom so with the Northern, He had to make them see that idolatry and the immorality that went with it were not for His people. After the return from exile the nation never fell into these sins again, even though they, like the Christian Church, still allowed many things that were wrong. Later, when the sinless Son came, God's people received an even more wonderful son-relationship in Him (John 1.11–13).

*Chapter* **14** *is worth reading as a sequel to this section.*

## Questions and themes for study and discussion on Studies 1–3

1. List some passages which show that God intends us to know Him.
2. How far can one distinguish in these and other passages between *knowing* and *knowing about*?
3. Consider the relevance of man's being made in the image of God for speaking of God as personal.

# CHARACTER STUDIES

## 4 : Nadab and Abihu

### Leviticus 10.1–11

No one knows the exact nature of the 'unholy fire' mentioned in this passage. The sharp judgement which fell on those who used it finds its moral justification in the nature of the task Aaron's two sons were called to perform. They stood at a critical point in the religious history of mankind, and those who hold the belief that a process of revelation was going on must grant the need for sharp lessons in matters vital to that revelation and its security.

Whatever Nadab and Abihu did, it was some act of irreverence, some error which revealed the lightness with which they held the intensely meaningful law and ritual committed to their hands. That which does present a greater problem to the modern reader of the Old Testament is Moses' command to Aaron to withdraw from the whole process and ritual of mourning for the two dead men. Is this a trait of hardness on Moses' part, or is it designed as a reinforcement of the sanctity of the Tabernacle, which had been violated by Nadab and Abihu?

The second suggestion may have some weight, but only if it is associated with Aaron's own fault. Aaron was responsible for the attitude of the two men which had led them to disaster. He had by his faulty and craven example encouraged their casual attitude towards divine things. When Moses ordered Aaron and the elders to wait in a certain place on Sinai (Exod. **24**.12–14), the two sons of Aaron saw their father give way to some pressure, perhaps from the Seventy, and

14

abandon the post of duty (Exod. **32**.1). When the multitude arose with impatient shouts of ingratitude towards the man who had led them out of Egypt, Nadab and Abihu saw their father quail before popular clamour and fail to exercise the authority which might have saved the people from the horrible situation into which they fell. When Aaron lied to Moses about the origin of the golden calf, Nadab and Abihu heard their father lie. It is little wonder that, so faultily trained, they themselves failed to obey the letter of some unrecorded ordinance. Hence the stern prohibition on their father.

# 5 : Caleb

## Numbers 13, 14; Deuteronomy 1; Joshua 14.6–15

The geography of the reconnaissance into Palestine is a little difficult to follow, and it could be that two separate parties covered the land, one much further to the north than the other. If this is so it would be a fair guess that Caleb led one party, and Joshua the other, and that Caleb's party returned first and gave its report. This would account for what appears to be a certain repetition between chs. **13** and **14**.

This is not of great importance. What matters is the reaction of the men of the two parties. The leaders, Caleb and Joshua, did not carry their men with them. We shall meet Joshua frequently in these chapters of biography. Caleb deserves a special look. But for the one fine hour of his return from the probe into Palestine he might never have been known.

Let it be promptly admitted that there was much to daunt the desert-tribes. Palestine was crowded. It lay across one of the great highways of trade and travel in the ancient world. It still does, and the news of almost every day, with Israel as a pawn and prize of East and West, as a barrier on the road to Africa, as a bridgehead into the Arab world, clearly demonstrates a truth of geography and of history.

The spies saw much to fill them with misgivings. Caleb, a quiet, simple, faithful man, if a guess may be hazarded about him, saw beyond the difficulties. He saw, like the rest, the sturdy little fortresses which studded the land. He was conscious, like the rest, of the power of Egypt which penetrated the area, ready to take a hand against all incursion from the hinterland. The vast difficulties which lay in the task of conquest were as obvious to him as to his timid companions. He simply had faith in the old promises made to the patriarchs.

Courage and faith overlap in the experience of the human personality. One feeds the other. If faith is lacking courage loses its tap-root. If courage is lacking no one can claim to possess faith. We should be glad of a closer look at this strong and valiant man. Our clearest glimpse is of many years later when the land was overrun and Caleb asks, strong as ever in old age, to be permitted to claim his inheritance. Courage in him proved itself in action. Faith, in a manner which would have delighted James, demonstrated its reality in deeds. So must it ever be.

## 6 : Korah

### Numbers 16

Those confident enough to divide an ancient document, on highly doubtful assumptions, into a composite story of several sources, imagine a threefold narrative in this chapter. There is no need, nor indeed, solid grounds, for this conjecture. Three bases of revolt are stated—first, that Moses and Aaron have usurped authority beyond their due, second, that the whole march was a failure, for the comparative security and plenty of their Egyptian bondage had been exchanged for the penury of the wilderness, on the promise of illusory prosperity, and thirdly, that the priesthood was no monopoly of the two brothers, but should be shared.

Admittedly, these three complaints sit awkwardly together, but the very fact throws what light the story may upon the character of Korah. He was obviously the typical demagogue, determined, if one charge failed or did not appeal, to be ready with another. It was a situation like that in Aesop's fable, where the wolf and the lamb drink from the same stream. Korah hoped to gain advantage. Protest is not always wrong, but a remark of Sir Thomas More often applies to such movements: 'Who does more earnestly long for change than he who

16

is uneasy in his present circumstances? And who run to create confusions with so desperate a boldness, as those who, having nothing to lose, hope to gain by them?'

The eminence of Moses was visible, and it is the way of some lesser spirits to envy all who stand above them. Korah had no sincerity, or the rabble-rousing charge of leading Israel into poverty and hardship would not have been added to the political complaints of Moses' autocracy and assumption of authority. Korah, encouraged by the adherence of the petty group who always gather round the disaffected, each for reasons of his own, and commonly for reasons less than honest, sought eminence for himself, not basic justice. Such people are one of the blights of democratic society. The envious man, said Horace, grows lean at his neighbour's success. Moses was no seeker of what men call success. His meekness and compassion are evident in this chapter. But Korah read others by his own preoccupations, and became, in the Bible, a warning for self-seekers. (Num. 26.9; Psa. 106.17; Jude 11; cf. Deut. 11.6.)

## * 7 : Balaam

### Numbers 22.1–31

The writers of the New Testament, with wider access to rabbinical tradition than we have, knew more of Balaam than the Old Testament reveals. For that reason it will be a good introduction to this strange story to read 2 Pet. 2.15; Jude 11; Jas. 4.4 and Rev. 2.14. These passages imply that Balaam was a hireling, selling spiritual things for money, and at the same time a cunning and effective diplomatist, who taught the foes of Israel those subtle devices of temptation and corruption by which the moral and spiritual strength of the people might be undermined. On such qualities the vigour of a nation depends, and the insight shown, albeit basely directed, is a pointer to the ability of this foreigner.

He came, significantly enough, from Pethor on the Euphrates, an old area of civilization, where some tradition of Abraham may still have lingered. He was no Canaanite, purveyor of grim superstitions, no wizard of some depraved pagan cult, but more likely, a man conscious of the obligations of higher religion, who knew God, had some regard for His guidance, was conscious of good, and the obligations of his spiritual calling. He sinned, in other words, against the light.

Hence the horror with which the New Testament writers regarded him. They saw his posterity in those who, for their own gain, for the ease of conformity, or in perversity, set out to modify Christianity, and to work out a compromise with the surrounding pagan world of the first century.

Up to v. 14 in the story of this chapter, Balaam has acted without obvious fault. He saw the right, sought God's will, and hearkened to the voice of his conscience. He had, nevertheless, his price, his weak point, and something in his message to Balak, or perhaps in the messengers' own report, betrayed this inherent weakness to a clever man. Hence the second embassy, and hence, it would appear, God's permission to accompany the envoys. God does not change His mind, and Balaam knew God's will in the matter. But Balaam was trying to cover that which he desired in self-will to do, with a convenient veil of piety. It was therefore in judgement upon him that God dismissed him on his way. Even then he was given, like Judas, a last chance to retreat to that which he knew was right. Dumb things have a voice, and an ass was used to call Balaam to heed his conscience.

## * 8 : Balaam's Concience

### Numbers 22.32–41

Even an ass, such is the irony of this passage, could see the stern presence which stood in Balaam's path. He was no doubt moving on in some trepidation, for at the outset of such pernicious enterprises, when an enlightened man moves obstinately forward in despite of conscience, the mind is apprehensive, and fear gnaws the heart. 'Half the wrong things men do,' wrote Robert Watson, 'are done, not in spite of conscience but with its dubious consent, when the first clear decision has been set aside.'

The remark is acute and fits the situation of Balaam exactly. He forced himself forward against the sharp verdict of his first clear enlightenment and found himself in the

18

hands of God, compelled to face the consequences of his chosen course. This is the clearest reading of the story, and takes into account the patterns of Hebrew thought in which God is regarded as the prime mover, because He established the complex of psychological laws which find expression in the situation. This was a matter glanced at when 'the hardening of Pharaoh's heart' was discussed in an earlier study (Vol. 2, Study 46).

Balaam's confession of sin (34) was no deep repentance. He was simply baffled in his hireling's course. A crafty programme sometimes escapes from the control of its initiator. God so governs that the very subterfuges and self-seeking of men can be woven into the plan of His purposes. That which a cunning and self-seeking man like Balaam begins to do in self-will cannot always be arrested at the point which the sinner determines. It is always wise to watch the beginnings of sin. We cannot 'with the deed trammel up the consequences', as we have already quoted, or contain in time and place that which we do amiss. Sin is like fire, apt to spread beyond control. Balaam's fundamental greed had landed him in the position which Judas found beyond all management. He was, rent between Almighty God, into whose hands he had fallen, and the prince in whose power his life was placed.

## 9 : Balaam the Prophet

### Numbers 23.1–26

Balak no doubt offered his sacrifices to Chemosh, sun-god of Moab, and now Balaam demands like sacrifice to Jehovah. He is the true type of the man who is well conscious of the truth, but unwilling, for love of some cherished advantage, to break his association with corrupt men. There is a pompousness about him which points to this damaging trait of character. With a royal air he bids the prince abide by the altar, and he himself withdraws with mysterious dignity to a vantage-point on the hills to meet his God.

From his high peak the hireling prophet could see the smudge of smoke from Balak's pitiable altar fires behind him, and far away to the east, in the clear desert air, he could look

over the sea of Israel's encampment. It required little insight
or special revelation to see with whom the future lay—with
the broken mountain tribe, or the advancing flood of sternly
moral nomads (22.41). This perhaps is why he was willing to
listen to the words which formed in his heart, and ready to
deliver Jehovah's message. His advantage obviously lay with
the newcomers, but the situation in which he found himself
was one which required some delicate handling. Balaam had
one advantage—his vast prestige with Balak. He played it
well, and thought in his base heart to win credit with God for
his self-interested faithfulness. Perhaps he had even heard of
Moses' advancing years, and envisaged the possibility of
stepping into so august a place. For those eaten by ambition,
the far skies are no limit. News travels fast among desert
tribes, and Balaam may have counted on the words of his
prophecy filtering down to the Hebrew camp. Certain it is
that the rich poetic words of his utterance brought him no
credit nor reward. They rose from evil motives.

Observe how in the very words notes of egotism and self-
defence break through. Balaam was none the less a man of
keen intellect, and caught, through all the fog of his self-
seeking, some vision of the great work God was beginning to
do in the deserts behind Jordan. God's words of himself, in
spite rose to his lips, and here again was a moment in which
he might have reached out and found salvation. It was like the
moment when Jesus washed Judas' feet.


## 10 : Balak

### Numbers 23.27–30

Read the whole chapter again, because here is a confrontation indeed. Obtuse superstition is set over against inspired
insight. And yet the victim of obtuse paganism is less blame-
worthy than the clever man who saw with perfect clarity the
shining truth, and yet failed to translate the vision into salutary deeds. The mummeries of heathendom are set in contrast with a breath of genuine prophecy, albeit on the lips of
one unworthy of uttering the words.

Observe Balak. He was the ruler of a poverty-stricken land.
The rain-laden winds from the Mediterranean had dropped

most of their beneficence by the time they reached the purple hill-country between Jordan and the wilderness, and the sacrifices of animals on the altars demanded by the expensive 'holy man' were not of the sort an indigent highland chieftain was likely to look on without thought of the cost. Animals were Balak's wealth.

The whole pathetic simplicity of the man is in view in the closing verses of the chapter. His conception of God determined his outlook. He had built himself a deity in his own image, making him, as the psalmist puts it, altogether like himself (Psa. 50.21). He thought of all beings as having their price. Balak was willing to meet all genuine accounts. In return he expected the goods for which he paid. And God was reckoned among his customers. The proper sacrifices had been made, but with no eye to any deeper meaning than that attaching to any business transaction. God must surely deliver the goods for which such payment had been faithfully made.

Balak's people had known defeat at the hands of the Amorites (21.26–30). Israel had defeated the Amorites, and had refrained from overrunning a broken Moab. Traverse had been refused, and now Balak was harvesting his folly. In the wretched hope that some return might yet be made for his outlay, he took Balaam to yet another eminence and had him prophesy. That is what Balaam did.

There is a lesson in the man. Even with the light of Christ before them there are those who regard their religion as a business transaction, and who 'tithe' to win prosperity, and trust God to rescue from self-chosen folly, and answer prayer according to specifications.


## 11 : Balaam Again

### Numbers 24

Regardless of expense, Balaam demanded similar sacrifices. Either this high-handedness was part of his self-exaltation before the chief, or perhaps he clung blindly to the thought that he might see some way out of his unsatisfactory performance. Or perhaps he still played the desperate double-game of favouring Israel in the guise of doing Moab's will. He was in a highly perilous situation, whichever way the truth lies, and whatever were the thoughts and motives in the subtle shaman's brain, no good clings to them, and no credit is owing to him.

Balaam, at this point, seems overwhelmed by God. Now, with no note of conciliation or excuse in mind for what to Balak appeared the basest of betrayals, Balaam spoke in wild poetry. Here again poured out the words which showed what Balaam might have been, had his life been clean, and had the genuine understanding which he had of the ways of God commanded his personal allegiance. He was, in fact, singularly well-informed about Israel, and even put into striking words a Messianic oracle (17).

Balak was utterly disconcerted. He clapped his hands, the common signal of despots for the devoted bodyguard to appear. No defender appears to have sprung to his master's side at the sound of the imperious signal. No doubt Balaam had been clever enough to take his royal employer to the eminence alone, and without the armed men who might, at the whim of the moment, have been ordered to deal with him. Helpless to order some incantation of cursing, Balak weakly bids the disobedient prophet be gone, and hears in return more self-righteous words, and another burst of prophecy.

Apparently Balaam did not permanently go. It might have been to his advantage to do so. The sequel shows that Balak was still under his influence, and he remained with base and consciously evil advice to win the advantage which Balak had in mind to confer upon him (11). The closing verse of the chapter appears to speak of separation. If so, it was temporary and the hireling returned to give nefarious advice. He may still have had in mind some liaison with Israel. Instead he won a name of infamy.

## 12 : Balaam's Baseness

### Numbers 25

Chapter 31 contains eight verses which round off the story of Balaam, and justify the traditions about the prophet which appear to have been known to the writers of the New Testament. He must have returned from his home to Moab neglecting yet another opportunity to extricate himself from a compromising and evil association. He was drawn back, by his own cupidity, to the place of temptation and disaster. God's patience went unregarded.

The chapter before us and its brief sequels make grim reading. Balaam, familiar with the base sexualities of the fertility cults of the land, cults which, with his genuine knowledge of the true God, he may well have despised, suggested to Balak that the promiscuity of some pagan ritual of the fields be used to seduce the men of Israel. Under Sinai the tribes had fallen into the temptation which such carnality could bring, and the stern code of separation, imposed upon the Hebrews, was primarily designed to form a barrier in such a world against the social and personal evils which the contemporary cults of obscenity and sexual perversion contained.

Hence the sanguinary repression of the popular outbreak. Moabite women, on some Dionysiac revel, must have invaded the camp. The weaker men among the people were drawn into the celebration. They were not the men among whom the destiny of Israel was safe. Hence the stern measures. But Balaam well understood the effectiveness of such an intrusion. To break the walls of morality which surrounded Israel, would ultimately be to break the nation. That law of decadence still functions. Therein lies the deep peril which confronts Christendom today. The walls are crumbling, and the only hope for Western Civilization is in the possible survival of a fortress in the midst, the Christian Church, not compromising, not tolerating the sundry Balaams who speak unctuously of another ethic than that which stands in Christ, but maintaining chastity and separation from the world's evil —such is the only hope for the race.

Balaam died as he had lived. To throw in one's lot with evil and evil men is to invite the fate which falls on such rebellion. It is poetic justice. Balaam had it in him to be a great man, a poet and a prophet. He might have found a place in history and a citizenship among the tribes. He desired this, in all probability, but he wanted it upon his terms, not God's.

**Questions and themes for study and discussion on Studies 4–12**

1. In what does irreverence consist?
2. Courage, cowardice, rashness and faith. Define each in relation to difficulty.
3. Rebellion. Is it ever justifiable?
4. Conscience and the Holy Spirit.
5. The self-defeat of obstinacy.
6. 'Sin and well-doing cannot be unfruitful.'
7. Balaam and Balak in their modern setting.
8. Christianity and prosperity.
9. False shepherds. See Milton's 'Lycidas' and John **10**.
10. What barriers preserve the Christian in an age of exaggerated sexuality?

# THE CHARACTER OF GOD

## A Holy and Righteous God

We now begin a section where it is hard not to be prejudiced. Starting from human experience, we tend to seize on aspects of God's revelation, and magnify or minimize them in isolation from the whole. Thus a human being often has a dominant characteristic that overrides his whole personality. Holiness can become priggishness, righteousness harshness, love a sloppy sentimentality, compassion spinelessness. God used different writers and different events to bring out aspects of His character, and, with the whole Bible in front of us, we bring these together so as to know the nature of God so far as we can comprehend Him. His holiness and righteousness are positive qualities, though they may appear to us as negative against the background of destructive sin.

## (a) Disclosed in Old Testament History

### 13 : The Hand of God in Destruction and Renewal

#### Genesis 6.9—7.4; 8.13–22

The historicity of the flood may be studied in the New Bible Commentary or the Tyndale Commentary on Genesis. Today people often say, 'Why doesn't God do something about all the violence in the world?' This portion shows that God has done something of this kind. The flood in a sense represents the ultimate judgement (Matt. **24**.38, 39; 2 Pet. **3**.3–7). At any moment God could wipe out violent and corrupt sections of humanity. The fact that He does not do so makes us realize again the Person-with-person influence.

The flood was one way of cleaning up corruption (6.11-13). The important sequel was the personal provision for the future. God's original purposes must be fulfilled through human beings rather than by repeated sudden judgements. Note the recapitulation of Gen. 1.26-30 in 8.17 and 9.1-7.

In the horror of destruction, God selects a group of human beings to carry through His purposes. Noah was one who reflected the righteous character of God (6.9; 7.1). With him God made the first recorded covenant (6.18), which not only saved him and his family, but which bound them into an even closer link with the purposes of God for the world. God and men pledged themselves to work for the total welfare of the created order without using the tool of total destruction (9.1-17), yet taking account of the inherent twist in human nature (8.21). Noah was soon to experience this twist in himself and in his sons (9.20-27).

*Consider the comment on Noah's relationship with God and man in Heb. 11.7.*


## 14 : God Sees a Spark of Righteousness

### Genesis 19.1-29

Here is another demonstration that God can cut out a cancer from the human race. If a similar cancer exists among us today, we cannot take the silence of God as an indication that He and we can ignore it (2 Pet. 2.6). A warning should be effective without constant repetition. If we find, as history and experience show, that the sins of Sodom sap the moral fibre of a nation, our common sense should see the judgement of God equally in this slower process. God has made us in such a way that persistent sin degrades us into an ever-increasing unlikeness to Himself, and piles up individual and social decay.

It is hard to draw a line between Lot's household and the people of Sodom. Lot had some awareness of the righteousness of God, and reacted righteously against giving way to the homosexuality of the city. Clearly this homosexuality was of the 'experimental' type and not the kind that calls for sympathetic understanding. But Lot's ideas were so befuddled by the crazy standards of the day that he was ready to substitute his daughters for his guests (8).

Lot took a tremendous risk when he deliberately chose Sodom as a desirable residence (Gen. 13.10–13). He tried to keep up his standards, and was constantly shocked by what he saw going on around him (2 Pet. 2.7 f.), as we are shocked by hysterical stories in the press. We may gather from v. 9 that he was known in the city for his criticisms of current morality, but his wife and family preferred the permissive society (14, 26). In the escape his wife kept hanging back until a shower of chemical ash caught her, just as the lava overwhelmed and encased the people of Pompeii (26).

God sent two angels to save Lot, and the prayers of Abraham undoubtedly had some weight. Abraham was realistic, and knew how rotten the city was (18.32). God worked a miracle to save Lot and his family. The Hebrew word translated *blindness* (11) occurs only here and in 2 Kings 6.18. In both places it is the equivalent of an implanted hypnotic suggestion, and could be translated *hallucination*.

*Consider how Christ used this story in Luke 17.28–37.*

## 15 : God's Character as His Will for Man

### Exodus 20.1–20

The Decalogue (Ten Commandments) is a fundamental declaration of spiritual and moral wholeness. It is not a set of external rules, but contains a dynamic inner life, as Christ showed in the Sermon on the Mount (Matt. 5.21 ff.). We must not suppose that God invented a set of rules to govern human life, as though He were inventing a game. These basic commands are a translation of His own character into human terms. We know this, not only because God specifically says, 'Be holy, for I am holy' (Lev. 11.44), but because, when He became Man, God the Son lived after the pattern that is here set out. The perfect values of a sinless human life are in harmony with the character of God. This is one way in which man is made in the image of God.

The Decalogue concerns our relation to God (3–11) and

the relationships that bind us all together in security (12–17). God Himself is to be the unifying key to the many facets of our life (3, Matt. **6**.24; Col. **3**.5). He cannot be portrayed in any material form that would draw our devotion (4, cf. Rom. **1**.23). Idols become God-substitutes, and God is jealous, i.e. rightly concerned, for our total devotion (5). When generation after generation drift into godlessness, each piles up an accumulation of divine, or natural, punishment (5, cf. Matt. **23**.34–36). In Ezek. **18**.14–18 we see that any generation may break with its evil predecessor and experience God's new life. Similarly there can be a cumulative experience of God's goodness from generation to generation (6).

As God's people we treat Him seriously (7). Since part of the image of God is spiritual capacity, we must take time to remember God together (8–10). This is the only commandment that is not reaffirmed after the resurrection of Jesus Christ, but its principle is taken up in the Lord's Day, in memory of the new creation (11) and redemption in Christ (Deut. **5**.15).

United families are unlikely to produce life-shortening revolutions (12). The right to life (13), family (14), property (15), and a good name (16), carries a corresponding duty to grant them to others. The final command reminds us to watch the inner springs if we would avoid damaging acts.

The physical phenomena enforced the seriousness of God's revelation (18–20). After this anyone could prove the truth of the revelation by experience, without seeing fire on the mountain.

*If love is the fulfilling of the law (Rom. **13**.10), how far does it need God's guidance for its application?*

# 16 : Principle of Obedience to God

## 1 Samuel 15

We approach this story with diffidence. Some have even held that Samuel, and not Saul, was the one who fanatically mis-understood God's will. Yet there is no indication that Saul was moved by humanitarian motives, as we might be, in sparing Agag and the animals.

With some things God worked towards a goal in the light

of man's current assumptions, rather than imposing His solution before man could see it for himself. This is Person acting on person. Christ asserted this principle with divorce and monogamy in Matt. **19**.8. Monogamy and permanent union, like peace, were inherent in the original creation, but, when 'hardness of heart' completely coloured man's outlook, God began again where man was, and slowly guided people to see His original plan. Slavery is another example.

God's use of war is harder for us to accept, but at that stage in man's cultural development war was a fact that everyone accepted. God's plan was peace, and David, who fought God's battles, was thereby debarred from building the Temple (1 Chron. **22**.8). Nearly every Messianic prophecy names the Messiah as the one who brings peace. Yet God's use of war in settling His people in the land was the best method, if not the only method, at that stage.

The concern of this chapter is not war, but obedience (11, 22). Amalek had formerly made an unprovoked attack on Israel (Exod. **17**.8–14), and a state of intermittent war existed between them (Exod. **17**.16; Deut. **25**.17–19; Judg. **6**.33; **7**.12), so Saul's attack cannot have been wholly unexpected (cf. **14**.48).

Saul turned his commission for total war into personal advantage, and, even after he had confessed his sin, he still clung desperately to his prestige (30). Meanwhile Samuel carried out capital punishment on Agag, whom he addressed as one who was known for his atrocities (33).

God's repentance (11) must always be interpreted in the light of man's change of attitude. It is God's reaction to a change from obedience to disobedience, and vice versa.

*Consider verse 29 : God remains consistent, but man may experience His dealings as repentant change.*

## 17 : God and the Family

### 2 Samuel 12.1–25

With David God began a fresh covenant line that was to culminate in the Messiah (2 Sam. **7**). Covenant does not mean favouritism in the sense that God turns a blind eye to sin. David had committed adultery with Bathsheba, and had virtually murdered her husband, Uriah the Hittite, whose name shows that he was a convert.

David may well have excused his action by reasoning that it brought comfort to a young wife whose husband, a rough foreigner, did not understand her. He could tell himself that Uriah might have been killed in battle even if he had not arranged for him to be in the real danger spot (11.15).

God broke into his sleeping conscience by an ostensibly true complaint that forced David, as chief magistrate, to make a decision that condemned himself (1–7). A king is not above the law of God, nor is anyone in authority in state, business, or family. David had lit a fuse that would fire off more than one explosion in his family. Son would fight with son and with father (10; ch. 13 ff.), and his own women would be publicly humiliated (11 f.; 16.20–22). One need not sort out how much was, as we say, God's direct judgement and how much the working out of His social laws, whereby family influences, good and bad, have more effect than advice and warnings.

Moreover the baby must die, and friends and enemies would see this as showing that God was not indifferent to David's adultery. If the full Hebrew text, without emendation, is kept in v. 14, we translate as the AV and RV, 'Because thou hast given great occasion to the enemies of the Lord to blaspheme', but there are difficulties, and the RSV and NEB are equally true in fact.

David's reaction is complete contrition and repentance, far deeper than the face-saving repentance of Saul, of which we read yesterday. Yet he hopes that prayer and fasting may avert the death of the baby. Once the child is dead, he accepts God's word and act as final.

Bathsheba was already his wife, and it would not have been right to divorce her. But David and others had to learn the hard way that, while polygamy was legally marriage and not extra-marital sex (as originally with Bathsheba), it was a system that God permitted but never commended. It almost always led to disruption, quarrels, and even violent death in the family.

*Psalm 51 so obviously belongs to this occasion that it is worth reading here.*

# 18 : Unholy History

## 2 Kings 17.1–28

We round off the historical records with the pathetic outline of Israelite history. Over some 700 years the defeated Canaanites gradually overcame their conquerors by the glamour of their religious and moral 'freedom', and enticed God's people out of the narrow way of holiness and righteousness. Very few Israelite kings and leaders set any effective example (8, 21), and some, like Ahab and Jezebel, even imported deities from countries round about (1 Kings **18**.19).

This passage is confirmed by contemporary prophets (13). There were shrines for the major gods and goddesses, as well as for the local spirits, in town and country (9–12, 16). If the gods demanded human sacrifices, the people offered their children (17), and they crashed the barriers of the supernatural by dabbling in the occult (17). Thus they parted company with the God of the covenant (15).

False religion is not just a matter of a different point of view. We know that the high place worship included acts of gross immorality, and in fact the women and men prostitutes there were called 'holy women' and 'holy men', according to the literal Hebrew of 1 Kings **14**.24, etc. They were dedicated to gods and goddesses, whose love scandals were told in popular legends. Their servants at the high places had the unholy holiness of the deities they served, and the worshippers, having tasted the excitement of free love, carried their laxity over into their daily lives. Looseness in one sphere infects all moral standards. Hence we have a practical demonstration of the need to see God as holy and righteous.

In 721 B.C. Assyria took the Northern Kingdom into exile, and settled others in their place (1–6). God spoke to these others in language that they could understand (25), so that they appealed for a priest to show them what the God of the land required (27). But when the priest came, probably bringing the so-called Samaritan Pentateuch, they merely took Jehovah into the pantheon of gods and goddesses that they already worshipped (33, 41).

The whole nation did not go into exile, and doubtless some were shocked into repentance by what had happened. A little later some, though not all, joined Hezekiah (2 Chron. **30**.5–11) and Josiah (2 Chron. **35**.17 f.) in keeping the Passover; for the time of Judah's captivity had not yet come (19).

*A poor god means a poor life (Rom. **1**. 19–32.)*


## 19 : Dangerous Future

### 1 Kings 8.22–53

We have now completed those historical passages that illustrate how God endeavoured to turn men and women from ways that led them further and further from His holiness and righteousness that they should be reflecting. On occasions He pointed the lesson by a sudden intervention, but at other times He spoke through a slow but significant unfolding of events with good men to interpret them. Our next three portions show two wise men turning the lessons of God's working into prayer.

The Bible never gives a one-sided presentation of any individual, because human beings are many-sided. Solomon was a not unusual mixture of intellectual wisdom (1 Kings **3**.12) and emotional folly (**11**.1–8). Perhaps the partial realization of his own weakness governed the course of this prayer at the dedication of the Temple, although undoubtedly he was familiar with the warnings and promises that God had given through Moses in Lev. **26** and Deut. **28**, with which this prayer may be compared.

Solomon has the clear view of God as the covenant God, who is utterly dependable (22–26). He knows that God cannot be confined to the Temple, but is aware of what all are doing all the time, since the whole universe is in His hand (27). Yet the Temple is a focal point for His presence with Israel (29).

If God is faithful in His promises, He is also faithful in His warnings. Hence Solomon lifts his eyes to the future course of history, and sees the people's need for mercy and forgiveness. God sees the secrets of every man's heart (31 f.). If the nation as a whole turns from God, He may use defeat in battle (33 f.), drought (35 f.), or pestilence (37–40) to bring them to their senses. Neither Solomon, nor we today, think that every disaster is God's judgement, but each one should make us seriously search our hearts and at least realize the brevity of life.

Solomon realizes Israel's mission to the nations (41–43). Hence the importance of their reflecting the character of God properly. In battle the Israelites must commit the justice of their cause to God (44 f.). Yet, with his awareness of human weakness (46), Solomon prepares sadly for a total collapse which would end in captivity. He sees that this need not mean complete destruction, but can be used for repentance and purification and a robust restoration that will be marked by holiness and righteousness (46–53, cf. Ezek. 36.24–29).

*Compare this prayer with Amos 4.6–13.*

## 20 : God Gives no Blank Cheque

**1 Kings 8.54—9.9**

Much of Solomon's prayer necessarily speaks of man's behaviour. Now he invokes the blessing of God, without whom all human behaviour is mere morality. God must ever be the prime mover to draw our hearts to Himself (56–58). Yet God does not draw us for our own sakes alone. He has called us, as He called Israel, to be those who reflect Him, so that outsiders will also be drawn to Him (59 f., cf. Gen. 12.2 f.; Zech. 8.22 f.). How important, then, to reflect God as He is, and not as the Canaanite deities (61)!

Next, Solomon offered the sacrifices. There was a single representative burnt offering, wholly consumed by fire, and signifying both propitiation and complete dedication (64). The main sacrifices were peace offerings, with accompanying cereal offerings (63, 64). These offerings were not useless slaughter, since the bulk of each peace offering was eaten by the worshipper and his family (Lev. 7.15 f.). Thus the dedication of the Temple was concluded with a festival meal for the vast crowds.

No voice came from heaven, but Solomon had a second vision of God that night (2, cf. 3.5 ff.). God spoke to him realistically. He granted Solomon's prayer, and promised that the Temple (3) and the monarchy (5) would be centres of His life and power. But, as Solomon realized in his prayer, this promise was not a blank cheque, but was tied to obedience, since otherwise Temple and king would be reflecting a false image of God (6–8), and God's concern for true righteousness would be better reflected in ruin than in continued survival (9).

We can now see the problem that continually faced God. He could not allow a degraded image of Himself to continue in His representatives, and therefore He had to show by the exile that He was not a God of doting favouritism. But once His people had gone into exile, pagans declared that their gods had conquered Jehovah (e.g. Dan. **5**.3 f.). So, once the nucleus of His people had seriously learnt their lesson, God brought them back, and from that time they did not again become involved in idolatry or gross immorality, which had been the characteristics of pre-exilic times.

*A New Testament equivalent is 1 Pet. **1**.14–22; **2**.9–12.*

## 21 : History as His Story

### Ezra 9

We have mentioned the return from exile. The exile of Judah and the destruction of Jerusalem was in 587 B.C. and the return in 537 B.C. The new Temple was finished in 516 B.C. Ezra was sent by the King of Persia about 60 years later to report on the state of Judah, and to enforce any necessary laws (**7**.14). He evidently held some such post in Persia as Secretary of State for Jewish Affairs, and he was a real man of God.

It was due to men like Ezra and Nehemiah that there was not a second landslide into Canaanite standards. Intermarriage, with all the emotional and relational ties that this brings, was beginning again, and even high officials of the State were involved (2). The matter was becoming a burning issue (**10**.1), but it was not too late to act. Someone like Ezra was needed to assess God's hand in history, and to see how He was pledged neither to overlook a deliberate flouting of His will, nor to refuse to rebuild the nation after true repentance. Solomon had looked ahead in uneasiness; Ezra had a long span of past history on which he had often meditated so as to perceive the character and ways of God.

Although he himself had a clear conscience, he identified himself in his prayer with the nation as a whole, as Daniel did before him (Dan. **9**) and as we ourselves must often do. Hence he uses the first person plural all through this prayer.

His prayer centres in confession (6, 7, 10, 13) and grateful remembrance of God's warnings which have a contemporary application (11 f.). He implies that the people are ready to put things right, since otherwise there would be no point in the prayer (13 f.), and in fact a proper committee of investigation was set up to deal with the situation as it stood (**10**.13 ff.). This was not the only public prayer that Ezra made, and on a second visit he read the Law aloud and led the people in a long covenant prayer, very similar in theme to this one (Neh. **9**.6–38), and again emphasizing God's character and acts.

He was not making a fuss about nothing. Canaanite immorality and religious ideas could easily have come in again, even though at this stage the question was marriage, not adultery, with unbelievers. Some might have argued that these marriages indicated a willingness for good-neighbour relationships. Doubtless also some of the leaders thought it desirable to be linked to influential and wealthy Canaanite families. Marriage, however, is more than a neighbourly contract.

*Intelligent prayer looks for the demonstration of God's character in the past and the present.*


## Questions and themes for study and discussion on Studies 13–21

1. Consider how compromises can produce unlikenesses to God in a Christian family.

2. What indications are there that the life of Jesus Christ on earth was after the pattern of the Decalogue, and what light does this throw on a link between divine and human righteousness?

3. In the light of the Sermon on the Mount, how far can one keep the letter of God's law without being transformed through a proper relationship with God?

4. 'To obey is better than sacrifice' (1 Sam. **15**.22). Why is this, if both are intended as part of the service of God?

5. 'Though the mills of God grind slowly, yet they grind exceeding small; Though with patience He stands waiting, with exactness grinds He all.' How far would David, Solomon and Ezra have agreed with Longfellow here?

# CHARACTER STUDIES

## 22 : Joshua Son of Nun

### Exodus 17.13, 14; 24.13; 32.17, 18; 33.7–11

An unobtrusive person has appeared five times in the closing chapters of Exodus. He is described only once, and with the utmost brevity: 'Joshua the Son of Nun, a young man . . .' (33.11). He appears in that same context to have been the guardian or keeper of the Tabernacle. We would be glad to know what went on in the mind of Moses' henchman during his lonely vigil in the beautiful place. It was, in fact, his second vigil. When Moses left the elders to wait and watch on the lower slope of Sinai, he moved up into the murk on the mountain with Joshua alone for company (24.13). It seems clear enough from the continuing narrative that Moses was alone on the mountain-top. When he came down to the dis-ordered camp, Joshua was again in his company. The situa-tion, therefore, appears to have been that Joshua waited alone for his master at some point higher up the slopes.

There may have been purpose in all this. Youth, for all the restless cries of the present century, is not in possession of all the answers. From immemorial time, man has sought to hand on his accumulated stocks of wisdom to the next generation. Youth must lay hold of the heritage, and age must learn when it is appropriate to stand aside and allow youth to take over. And, save in changeless tribal communities, like those of the Australian aborigines, youth commonly takes what age gives, and interprets it in the light of new experience, but youth must beware lest, in its natural impatience, it changes tradition too soon and in the light of experience too tenuous and too brief.

Joshua speaks only once in the few passages of narrative in which he appears. He knew that Moses prayed for him. He knew that Moses was seeking to pass on his immense experience. It is an enormous privilege for a young man to serve an apprenticeship of service under a man of surpassing strength, goodness and knowledge. They are wise who recognize the worth of such a rare tutelage, and make every endeavour to learn. The passing years terminate all things, and nothing more rapidly than that brief phase of life called youth. Joshua recognized this fact, and in his silence and, at times, enforced withdrawal, allowed the lessons of his fellowship with the great to sink deep into his spirit. We shall follow Joshua's progress, and it will be interesting to observe those traits of character which came to him from Israel's first chief and legislator.

## 23 : Joshua Takes Over

### Deuteronomy 3.21–29; 34.1–12; Joshua 1

'Show me the man you honour,' said Thomas Carlyle, 'and I will show you the man you are, for it shows me what your ideal of manhood is, and what kind of a man you long to be.' Through the story of the desert wanderings of Israel, Joshua has appeared consistently and unobtrusively at Moses' side. He is the very image and ideal of the faithful servant and loyal officer. It is obvious that in Moses, Joshua saw greatness. It is equally obvious that he would measure himself against Moses' superb equipment of mind and spirit, his education in all the culture of a great imperial race, trained in a royal household for the tasks of leadership, and divinely commissioned in his office.

Inevitably, Joshua would learn to rely on his hero and his leader. He would draw into the fabric of his own personality traits of Moses' character which would aid and steady him, but which at the same time would check the free and full development of his own characteristic attitudes and personal worth. He would find dependence upon the older

37

man's wisdom and swift insight becoming a part of his daily habit.

In such situations there comes the moment of loneliness and challenge. A parent dies, a leader is removed, and the next generation stands suddenly in the front rank, with no one to command, no one to lead, and a task demanding action awaiting.

Hence the word to Joshua. The word 'success' occurs in Josh. 1.8. It is said that this is its only appearance in all the vocabulary of the Authorised Version (KJV). The word suggests what was the nagging question in Joshua's mind: 'Can I do it?' 'Is the task beyond me?' Montesquieu remarked once that 'success depends on knowing how long it takes to succeed'. Joshua had at least the clear indication that it was going to demand concentration (8) and perseverance, and both, in the conquest of any land set before us, are worth more than talent and opportunity. Not that Joshua was without talent and opportunity. He was an able and a mature soldier. His host stood poised on the frontier of conquest, desert-hardened. He needed, none the less, a strengthening of spirit, and above all a sharp awareness that the leader who had gone from the camp was not the only source of command, direction and guidance. We shall look at this matter more closely in the next study.

## 24 : Joshua's Encouragement

### Deuteronomy 31.7, 8, 22, 23; 1 Corinthians 16.13

Read Joshua 1.1–8 again. It is possible to see in what was said to Joshua, the attitude of mind in which, at this dawn of a new day in his people's history, he looked across the twisting river to the blur of green where Jericho's fortress walls stood among the palms.

He felt weak, fearful and untaught. Then came, the very echo of the dead Moses' voice, the command to be strong (cf. Deut. 31.22 f. with Josh. 1.6). Joshua was no weakling. No man can answer for his courage who has never been in danger, but a trumpet call can nerve the spirit, and Joshua's call came from a Voice he knew to be the word of God for him, and which quite uncannily took up the very words of the one who was never far from Joshua's memory at this hour of crisis. The task was so similar. The Jordan lay across the path as the Red Sea once had lain. Unknown tracts lay ahead, and nothing so tries courage as the unknown. Joshua felt the pull of fear.

'What is strength,' Milton asked, 'without a double share of wisdom?' Milton, scholar as he was, probably had a verse of Horace, the Roman poet, in his mind: 'Force, reft of counsel, falls of its own weight.' To storm across the river, and in a rush of fanatic bravery to assault the walls of Jericho, was no answer to the problems of the day. Joshua needed supremely what he had known so long—wisdom. Moses was gone, but Moses' law remained, and it was Moses, as much as God, which Joshua found in the code which was now the possession of the people.

And so emerges the clear outline of a good man's character —a man conscious of his needs, and of the qualities he lacked, a man who was aware of weakness and inadequacy, and of his own defects of wisdom and judgement, but a man utterly committed to the vast work in hand, prepared to listen, to obey his God, to study to do all things according to God's will. God asks no more of man. Such a man He can use. Josh. 3 and 4, which should be read, clearly show the steadied personality of the leader of Israel, the new man taking shape.

## 25 : Nun

### Deuteronomy 4.9, 10; 6.7, 20–24; 11.18–21; 32.46

A character too likely to be forgotten must find a place, if not in our study, at least in our imagination, before we leave the first pages of the story of Joshua. Joshua was 'the son of Nun'. The influence of Moses in the life of his faithful deputy is rightly stressed, but long before Moses picked Joshua to be his lieutenant, another man, and perhaps a woman, played a decisive part in the life of the youth who was to lead Israel.

Observe the passages from Deuteronomy set out above. It was almost an obsession with Moses to hand on the great tradition. It may have been a memory of his own parents, or of whoever it was who saw to it that the prince in Pharaoh's household should not be cut off from the memory and calling of the race to which his blood belonged, which God used to prompt this deep preoccupation. At any rate, Nun, the father of Joshua, must have obeyed.

We know nothing about him. He is a mere name, like the parents of many another man, who, for good or ill, have left a mark upon the pages of human history. We can only judge Nun by Joshua his son. Francis Quarles wrote three and a half centuries ago: 'In early life I had nearly been betrayed into the principles of infidelity; but there was one argument in favour of Christianity which I could not refute, and that was the consistent character and example of my own father.'

Parents are sometimes unaware of how deep and abiding an influence they have on the character of their children. It is a fair guess that Nun, for all the obscurity which surrounded his earthly life, was a faithful man. So it is with life. It is not given to all to stand in the blaze of prominence. The occasion makes for fame, but does not produce the worth on which fame rests, as Gray remarked to those that lay in Stoke Poges churchyard:

> Some village Hampden, that with dauntless breast
> The little tyrant of his fields withstood;
> Some mute, inglorious Milton here may rest,
> Some village Hampden, that with dauntless breast

The great men of the world do their deeds and win their laurels. Again and again, it is a wife, a parent, a teacher, a friend, unknown to the record, who has made them what they are.


## 26 : Rahab

### Joshua 2.1–24; 6.17, 22–25; Hebrews 11.31; James 2.25

Rahab had a house which was part of the town wall of Jericho. She may have been an inn-keeper, and 'harlot' could be a pejorative term used for people engaged in this tavern trade, a term, no doubt, at times justified. Jericho lay on a trade-route, and it seems likely enough that the spies who came in with the jostling crowds would wear some fashion of disguise, and follow the itinerant merchants and tradesmen to such hostelries and accommodation as catered for the passing visitors to the valley.

Or Rahab could also have been a temple courtesan whose spirit sickened of the base religions of Canaan which demanded her body's service as a ritual of some foul fertility cult. The fact that Rahab knew all about the great movement of nomadic tribesmen across the Jordan reveals two facts—first, that there was considerable traffic in and out of Jericho, and secondly, that a woman of Jericho was accurately enough informed about the God of the strangers to find in her own mind the pull and urgency of a call to nobler living.

Rahab was a woman of resource and intelligence. She knew how to outwit the royal police, and bravely risked her all in hiding the spies on her flat roof beneath the bundles of flax. She drove a shrewd bargain with the fugitives. It was to include all her family. Her scheme of retreat similarly showed her intelligence. She had sent the pursuers off to the fords of Jordan five miles away across the valley floor. She directed the spies westwards towards the wall of hills which define the Jordan plain towards Judea. Visible from the mound of Jericho is the traditional Mount of the Temptation, an arid wall of rock which was probably 'the hills' of Rahab's phrase.

Rahab had given the spies priceless information. 'What is the use of concrete if the will is weak,' sneered Hitler after Munich in 1938 when his staff marvelled at the toughness of the abandoned Czechoslovakian fortifications. Rahab had shown a Jericho in no condition to withstand the Hebrew onslaught. Battles are won and lost in the minds of men. In all the strife of life it is morale which counts. Now look and wonder at Matt. 1.5.

## 27 : The New Joshua

### Joshua 3 and 4

To read these chapters attentively is to gain a conception of some toughening in the spirit of Israel's leader. There is a dash of Moses' decisiveness about him. He had been bidden 'be strong and of a good courage', and has obeyed the behest. 'There is nothing,' said Hazlitt, 'more to be esteemed than a manly firmness and decision of character. I like a person who knows his mind and sticks to it, who sees at once what, in given circumstances, is to be done and does it.' This is Joshua exactly, as he organizes the crossing of Jordan. He has his host under perfect discipline. The Jordan runs dry, and the machinery of this provision was such as has been seen in the present century, the damming of the stream by earth-falls in a narrow ravine through which the course cuts, further to the north.

Then there was the strange and silent marching round the city, an uncanny proceeding, which could have been spoiled by one man breaking rank, or replying to the shouts of derision and insult which would undoubtedly come from the watching Canaanites on the wall. Joshua could risk the strange manoeuvre only if he knew that his army could be trusted to carry out a command which it was impossible to explain to them, and which to many hard-headed soldiers in the ranks must have appeared the folly and absurdity which the watching Canaanites probably described it in ribald terms.

Joshua had clearly been accepted by a people accustomed to obey the commands of Moses, a 'stiff-necked' people, not given to an easy docility. It must betoken a quality in the man himself which commanded obedience. Sir Philip Sidney said: 'A brave captain is as a root out of which, as branches, the courage of the soldiers doth spring.' Here are the captain and the army which take shape before us in those chapters of strife. Moses' labours were bearing fruit. Moses' successor was 'entering into his labours'.

Note 4.24. It explains a good deal in Joshua's stormy story. A dominant idea held his mind. He wished to magnify God—in a word, to make God, and not himself, appear great in the eyes of the people. Joshua was a man of briefer speech than his old chief Moses, but the purport of his message was the same. No people prospers who degrades or dims the image of God.


## 28 : King of Jericho

### Joshua 5 and 6

We may allow ourselves the liberty, as we look at the men and women of the Bible, to probe in imagination a little behind the text, and picture those who do not stand clear cut in the story, and visible in their detail. We sought in this way to see Nun, the father of Joshua. What of Joshua's enemy, the prince who ruled Jericho?

There is little said about this petty Canaanite chief. He was obviously alert for peril, and in some command of the situation inside the walls of his fortress-town. He was immediately informed of the arrival of the strangers at Rahab's house, and promptly despatched an investigating team. Beyond the recording of these details of promptitude and decision, the Bible has nothing to say.

Palestine was an Egyptian buffer area. From time immemorial until today, the power on the Nile has sought control over the long narrow strip of territory between the Rift Valley and the sea, and these centuries were a period of dominant, though fluctuating, Egyptian influence. The small fortress towns of Palestine were in the hands of chiefs who owed allegiance to Pharaoh.

In the Tell el Amarna letters are numerous communications from places in Palestine begging for help from Egypt against some form of nomad invasion. If Garstang's earlier date for the Exodus and the invasion of Palestine could be otherwise established, these pleas could undoubtedly be referred to the dilemma of chiefs like the ruler of Jericho, left without resource against the Hebrew attack during a period of Egyptian preoccupation at home.

We cannot here go into the question of the date, but the letters from Palestine do speak of the fear which must have been abroad in southern Canaan, whatever the date. For example, Arad-Hiba, king of Jerusalem, writes of people called 'the Habiru', who are on the move: 'They are capturing the fortresses of the Pharaoh,' he says. 'Not a single governor remains. All have perished. Zimrida of Lachish has been killed. Let Pharaoh send help.' And so on. Such was the dilemma in Jericho, whether these strange documents refer to the actual attack of Joshua on the land, or to some similar inroad a century and a half earlier. The king of Jericho, in his small heat-ridden town, amid a servile population, cursed by sombre and sanguinary gods, must have felt a wretched man indeed.

## 29 : Achan

### Joshua 7; 1 Chronicles 2.7

Example, said Edmund Burke, 'is the school of mankind. They will learn in no other.' And it was Kant who set down the ethical principle: 'So act that your principle of action might safely be made a law for the whole world.' Achan cared nothing for principle or example. He set his family a grim pattern of covetousness, and disobedience. At this crisis in the nation's history, discipline, and absolute willingness to obey, were vital. Achan could not see it so. No man is so insignificant as to be sure that his example will do no harm.

Moreover, Israel was moving into the forefront of history with a moral law superior to anything the world had so far known. True, in the Euphrates Valley, Hammurabi had codified the law. The people of Haran and the Hittites had their legal codes. No people had anything quite like the Ten Commandments, nor a Law which referred all sin and righteousness to God alone. And here, on the very threshold of a great move forward in the nation's history, when, as the word to the leader had it (1.8, 9), all success depended on the moral stamina which social righteousness could give, one man opts out, and abandons the very source of all the nation's hope for strength and victory. Achan knew better, he thought, than Joshua and Moses' Law.

He had no care for the future, no concern for his family, involved, as he had seen in the desert and at the time of Korah's rebellion, in the parent's sin. A corrupt environment lay across the people's path. A culture, shocking in its decadence, was symbolized by the material wealth of Jericho. Joshua sought a ritual of separation to which all those who went forward to battle were called to commit themselves. Hence, as with Ananias and Sapphira, the stern punishment. There are high moments of history when all is at stake.

The Septuagint translation of 7.25, 26, which, of course, could represent an ancient text, omits reference to the destruction of family and goods, and since also the pronouns 'him' and 'them' can easily be confused in Hebrew, some have thought that the instructions of 7.15 were not, in the end, carried out. The story, whatever the end was, is vivid evidence of the deep feeling for the solidarity of the community held by Israel at this point of history.

**Questions and themes for study and discussion on Studies 22–29**

1. What can youth learn from old age?
2. 'When I am weak, then I am strong.'
3. 'Like father, like son.'
4. Defeat accepted is defeat assured.
5. Does the job make the man or the man the job?

# THE CHARACTER OF GOD

## A Holy and Righteous God

## (b) Declared in Psalm and Prophecy

### 30 : Vindication by the Righteous God

#### Psalm 7

The occasion of this psalm is unknown. The Cush of the title is not mentioned in the history. The meaning of *Shiggaion* can only be guessed at, but it could signify a *lament*. The psalm is from a Davidic collection, and may well be by David himself, presumably before he became king. We can gather something of the background from the contents.

The psalmist has been seriously slandered, and is in danger of lynching, or perhaps ostracism (1 f.). He is accused of treacherous injury to a friend as well as to an enemy (3 f.). Treachery was a major crime, and the psalmist's defence must be viewed in the light of the specific charge against him. He appeals to God for vindication, not claiming to be sinless, but to be innocent of this particular accusation (6–11).

At the same time his thoughts are drawn out over a wider field. It is because God is holy and righteous that David can make this appeal, but His holiness and righteousness are concerned with all that is wrong (11). There is more than one Cush in the world, as was shown at the trial of Jesus Christ. Cush finds the standards of God's people a perpetual handicap and rebuke for his plans. He schemes and plots his way through life (14), but God has so made things that he is often trapped by his own methods (15 f.). We see this in various

46

ways today—in retaliation against brutality, in the collapse of ruthless businesses, and in the crash of petty, and not so petty, criminals. Not every criminal suffers precise retribution in this life, but life moves in this direction, and is a proof that God is concerned here and now, and will be more plainly concerned at the final judgement (7 f.).

Meanwhile the Christian trusts God even when he is passing through undeserved darkness as David was. He searches his heart, so that he may be clear of sin so far as he can tell, as well as clear of specific charges (Psa. **19**.12 f.).

*Compare this psalm with 1 Cor. 4.1–4.*


# 31 : Call to the Nations

## Psalm 99

This is the last of a group of psalms (**93–99**) that celebrate the reign of the Lord on His throne. They build up the picture of God who is concerned with the actions of His people and of all nations of the world. Although at present He rules over rebels, the day will come when He manifests Himself to establish total righteousness,

This present psalm is an appeal, first, to all nations to bow to the rule of God (1). This means at least recognizing that He is concerned with moral issues. But for the true knowledge of God the psalmist comes back to the revelation that He has given to Israel and the Jews. In the Tabernacle and Temple He manifested His presence over the cherubim (1), in the Holy of Holies (Exod. **25**.22; 1 Kings **8**.7–10), and also used the cherubim as guardians of His throne in heaven (Psa. **18**.10; Ezek. **10**.1, 4, 18–20).

So Zion is to be God's centre to draw all peoples to Him (2 f.). These peoples will see Him as very different from their own gods, for He is holy. Note the repetition of this word in vs. 3, 5, 9. They must see God's hand in Israel's history (6 f.), learning the way in which He raised up priests and prophets as His mouthpieces. In personal relationship these men spoke to God (6), and He spoke to them (7). What He revealed was not simply food for the mind, but guidance for life (7).

In case the nations accuse God of favouritism, the psalmist points out that the way of God's servants is both enviable and exacting. They proved that God answers prayer and that He forgives, but they also suffered the consequences of disobedience (8). Moses and Aaron died without entering the promised land (Num. **20**.12). Samuel's lapse probably lay in appointing his sons as judges although they were bad men, thus precipitating the people's demand for a king (1 Sam. **8**.1–6).

Those of us Christians who are Gentiles have become incorporated into Israel's history; e.g. Abraham is our 'father' (Gal. **3**.29). We also use the Jewish Old Testament as part of our Sacred Book of God's revelation. Although earthly Jerusalem does not belong to us, this was a sacramental shadow of the heavenly Mount Zion, to which we belong (Heb. **12**.22–24). In this visible city of the old economy the blessings of the heavenly Zion were foreshadowed and, in part at least, enjoyed. Our God is the One of whom this psalm speaks. As the holy and righteous One, He is to be approached with awe and reverence (Heb. **12**.28 f.).

*Read at least one other psalm in this kingdom group* **(93–99)**.


## 32 : The Holy One of Israel

### Isaiah 6

In these notes so far we have assumed that we know the meaning of *holy* and *righteous* when the terms are used of God. The full significance emerges in the call of Isaiah. We saw in the notes on 2 Kings **17**.1–28 that the high-place prostitutes were called *holy*. This shows that originally the word had a meaning of *set apart as dedicated to a deity*, and it was without moral content. In the Law the term is frequently used of people, things, places and occasions, set apart for God or used by Him. Occasionally it is used of God Himself (e.g. Exod. **15**.11; Lev. **19**.2).

It was especially through Isaiah, in all parts of the book that bears his name, that God revealed Himself under the title of the Holy One of Israel. The title in its various contexts signifies His transcendence, His purity, and His covenant relationship with His people, who, as His people, should be like Him in character.

We cannot say why Isaiah's call is not recorded at the opening of his book, but this call must have dominated his life and teaching. He sees the transcendent glory of One who is separated, or 'holy', from man, and who is omnipotent over all the earth (1–4). Isaiah's reaction is in moral terms. It is not simply his own littleness that crushes him, but his unlikeness to God, and the unlikeness of people who professed to be in covenant relation with God (5).

The awful gulf is there, but God bridges it by removing Isaiah's unholiness with a coal still glowing from consuming sacrifices for sin (6 f.). Then as God's personal representative he can be commissioned to go to those who are still unholy and unrighteous (8–10). The wording of the commission sounds strange to us, but to Hebrew thought it means that Isaiah was faced with God's inevitable law that continual rejection hardens. Warnings to repent and be holy might be repeated again and again, but God saw that the people were so little prepared to listen that they would stiffen themselves even more in resistance to God. The result would be drastic judgement on the whole State (11 f.). But the gospel of God's holiness has promise as well as warning. Within the nation, ripe for destruction, would be an inner nucleus, a *holy* seed, from which fresh life would emerge (13).

*Compare the use of the term 'holy' in 1 Pet. **1**.15 f.; **2**.5, 9, with its use in Isa. **6**.*

## 33 : Substitutes for God-likeness

### Isaiah 1

Now that we have embarked on the prophets, we shall see that all of them are concerned with the enormous contrast between potential likeness to God, i.e. holiness, and actual behaviour. This chapter is a sad introduction to all that follows. If God is 'the Holy One of Israel' (4), the purpose of His special relation with Israel is that they too may be holy. Israel, however, has lost the meaning of belonging to the true God (2–4). Thus the nation is sick with sin (5 f.) and battered by invasion (7 f.), probably the invasion of **7**.1 f. and 2 Chron. **28**.5–21. Jerusalem has become like the fragile huts of branches and leaves that were put up temporarily as a refuge for the watchmen who guarded the crops (8). Isaiah sees hope only in a nucleus, that remnant of which God spoke at the end of his inaugural vision (6.13).

No doubt his hearers are surprised at being characterized as Sodom and Gomorrah (10). They have entirely misinterpreted what it means to belong to the covenant God. They think that His requirements can be fully met by an abundance of offerings and by punctilious ritual (10–15). Isaiah is not trying to sweep away the prescribed sacrifices, any more than he is trying to abolish prayer (15), but likeness to God means something far more fundamental. For man it involves both negatives and positives, putting away and absorbing with a view to action (16–23).

So the call is to meet God face to face, and to talk and listen realistically about sin and its promised removal (18), and about power for obedience (19). The alternative is for the nation to learn the hard way, when God sanctions exile with a view to purification (24–26). There must be a clear cut distinction between the repentant nucleus and the persistent rebels (27 f.).

We have thought several times of the Canaanite nature-worship, and there is a reference to this in vs. 29 f., together with a reference to an eastern religion in which miniature 'window boxes' of quick growing herbs were cultivated in honour of Tammuz, or Adonis. The chapter closes with the reminder that insolent strength that defies God can bring nothing but its own destruction (31, cf. 2.6–11).

*How far is the promise of v. 18 absolute and how far does the chapter indicate man's side? What does the New Testament say?*


## 34 : Substitutes for God's Truth

### Jeremiah 7

Jeremiah's ministry was approximately 100 years after that of Isaiah, but what he says is almost exactly the same. In Isaiah's time King Hezekiah had exerted a good influence on the nation, and God brought about an unexpected deliverance for Jerusalem from the armies of Assyria (Isa. 37.14–37). Yet neither leaders nor people rose to the occasion as the living nucleus of which Isaiah had spoken (see Isa. **6**). By the time of Jeremiah they were sliding rapidly downhill again, and Babylon had taken the place of Assyria. Once again, a good king, Josiah, forced a reformation on the people (2 Kings **22, 23**), but failed to change their hearts.

So God repeats the well-worn message. People still pinned their faith to externals, and comforted themselves with the possession of the Temple of the Lord (4). But their very presence was desecrating it, since its meaning lay not in stones and metal but in being the meeting place of God and man, and man was completely out of harmony with God both in his negatives and in his positives (5–11).

Somehow the people must have their pattern of thinking broken, in order to see what true relationship with God really is. Once, God had allowed the Philistines to destroy the sanctuary at Shiloh and capture the ark (12, cf. 1 Sam. **4**). Now, by sanctioning the destruction of Temple and city and the exile of the people, He will show that His true requirements are not linked to a superstitious attachment to externals (13–15).

Idolatry also was rife with its alternatives to the covenant God, and Ishtar-Venus worship was carried on in Jerusalem (17 f.). It is not simply that God is insulted by idolatry, but He knows that idolatry degrades the worshipper (19). The words that follow (21–23) must be seen in their context. Jeremiah does not deny the divine command to sacrifice, but denies the interpretation that sacrifice is an end in itself. Sacrifice was planned to go hand in hand with repentance, and to be the expression of a grateful heart. It was to be the handmaid of obedience, not a substitute (24–26).

Once obedience, discipline and truth have gone (28), there is little in common between God and man, and there can only be rejection of the nation (29). Where they sacrificed their children to Molech (31 f., cf. **32**.35) they will themselves be slaughtered by the invaders (32–34). There is no note of hope here, but Jeremiah, like Isaiah, knew that out of the ruins would come a renewed people (e.g. ch. **31**).

*What message has this chapter for a nominally Christian nation?*

## 35 : Ruin that God will not Prevent

### Ezekiel 7

While Jeremiah was drawing towards the end of his ministry
in Jerusalem, Ezekiel was beginning his in Babylonia. He
had been taken there with King Jehoiachin in 597 B.C., while
Jerusalem was still left standing. He directs the first part of
his book to the state of Jerusalem and its approaching doom.
It is a tragic comment that the only way in which the people
could 'know that I am the Lord' (4) would be by experiencing
God-sanctioned disaster to the full. In this way they would
see that, as the people of God, they could not remain in a
mass of abominations (1–9).

The same abominations run through the whole of Israel's
history, and prophet after prophet takes them up. Injustice,
pride, violence (10 f.) may be general terms, but they were all
translated into practical action (23). Idolatry also was rife
(19 f., cf. 6.1–7; 8.1–18). So now final destruction approaches
as the Babylonians hem the city in. As the siege is pro-
longed, the choice is famine, pestilence, violent death, or the
plight of refugees and prisoners (15 f.). All the securities of life
now vanish into insecurity. The army melts away (14, 17); fear
reigns (18); money is worthless (19); valuables are looted (20,
21); houses and shrines are wrecked (24).

There may come a point at which an appeal to God is too
late (26, cf. Jer. 7.16). The fact is that there is no repentance,
but the appeal for a vision (26) is like a visit to a fortune-
teller, which does not involve any spiritual or moral commitment. The priest has lost his grip of the book, and the elders
are too bewildered to guide the nation's life; so the mass of
the people is paralysed with panic (27).

*Consider Jer. 5.26–31 as a parallel to some of this chapter.*


## 36 : God's Will and the Common Conscience

### Amos 1.1—2.3

Chronologically we move back some 160 years from
Ezekiel. The date of the earthquake is unknown, but the
event was long remembered (1, cf. Zech. 14.5). The three
major (longer) prophets each have a set of messages for

Gentile nations, and the shorter book of Amos has a similar set in this opening section.

This raises the important question of what God expects from those who do not have the revelation of His Word (2). Rom. 1.19–23 says that the universe points sufficiently clearly to an eternal Creator to block the way to crude idolatry and moral irresponsibility. Through Amos God attacks atrocities which should shock the sensibilities of all mankind. Thus in a sense this chapter shows that an honest humanism can go some way with revealed religion.

The formula of 'three and four' is merely a Hebrew expression of repetition (cf. Prov. 30.18, 21). Benhadad of Syria, son of Hazael (2 Kings 13.24), had evidently carried out an invasion of Gilead, and had crowned it by butchering the prisoners under heavy spiked sledges (3 f.). Gaza, one of the Philistine city-states, had run a slaving raid for easy money (6, 7). The naming of the other Philistine cities (8) suggests that they also were involved to some extent.

Tyre had behaved similarly, but with the additional crime of breaking a treaty (9). Edom was frequently treacherous, and, as descended from Esau, was particularly hostile to the descendants of Jacob. The actual incident of v. 11 is not known, but it was similar to what happened when Edom took advantage of the Babylonian sack of Jerusalem (Obad. 10–14). The atrocity of the Ammonites (13) has been paralleled in ancient and modern times, and is one of the horrors that goes far beyond straight warfare. Moab's crime (2.1) sounds small in comparison with the others, and yet desecration of the dead by insult to the corpse is a conscience-shocking act.

Each nation comes under judgement. In fact, all of them were destroyed as nations, with the exception of Syria, which has retained its identity down the centuries. Kir (5) has not been identified, though it is also named in Amos 9.7 as the place from which the Syrians had come. Thus the predicted exile could mean that, as we say, Syria 'goes back to square one'. This is not as forced as it sounds, since Hos. 8.13 speaks of Israel's exile to Assyria as a return to Egypt. God evidently gave Syria a fresh chance of survival.

*When modern crimes shock the non-Christian, how far is this common conscience of mankind a reflection of man's original creation in the likeness of God?*

53

# 37 : Sin Against God's Revealed Truth

## Amos 2.4–16

Amos was a foreign missionary, in the sense that he came from Judah to preach to the northern kingdom of Israel. He had doubtless gained a favourable hearing as he denounced the hated foreigners, as can happen in protests today. Since there was always tension between Israel and Judah, his denunciation of Judah (4 f.) would also be cheerfully accepted. The charge against Judah is different, since Amos no longer speaks of the common conscience, but of the rejection of revealed truth. In these days we also must take this seriously. It is all too easy to dismiss the Bible as secondary provided that we react against the general evils in the world. Likeness to God is built through God's revelation of Himself in Scripture, and not simply on feeling.

Since Israel (as well as Judah) had inherited the Pentateuch, some of the crowd may have wondered what would come next, and in the remainder of the chapter Amos lashes his hearers in charge after charge. He highlights unscrupulous business methods (6, 7), religious prostitution at the high places (7, 8), the retaining of warm clothes taken in pledge for their own use (8) in defiance of Exod. 22.25–27, and the claiming of spurious damages so that they can drink away the fines at the local high place (8).

They have not heeded the divine pattern of history that Moses and Joshua recorded (9 f.), and they would not listen to contemporary prophets nor to Nazirites, who witnessed to God's serious call by protesting against the encroachments of debilitating luxuries like heavy drinking (11 f.). The uncut hair of the Nazirite (meaning *separated*) acted as a kind of badge to show friends and acquaintances that they were pledged to total abstinence. (For their vow, see Num. 6.) The Israelites forced them to break their vow, and silenced the prophets (12), thus stifling the critical voice of God.

So once again there comes the familiar threat of judgement. We must be growing tired of the word, but it is not purposeless destruction. All these sins and indulgences sap a nation's strength. They become heavy and torpid (13), and lose normal human reactions (14–16), so that they are an easy prey when the day of reckoning comes.

*Is there a place for some kind of voluntary Christian Naziritism today as an expression of some aspect of God's calling ?*

## Questions and themes for study and discussion on Studies 30–37

1. Which actions that these chapters denounce as out of harmony with God are found to any extent in our own country?

2. Check in a concordance the references to God as the Holy One of Israel.

3. Compare the call and commission of Isaiah with that of Jeremiah (1) and Ezekiel (1.1—3.11) in respect of their reaction to God's manifestation of Himself.

4. When can 'natural' events be regarded as the judgement of God?

# CHARACTER STUDIES

## 38 : Joshua Relives the Past

### Joshua 8

The future of a country is secure only in the hands of those who hold a regard for the past. It was Washington who once said: 'We ought not to look back unless it is to derive useful lessons from past errors, and for the purpose of profiting by dearly bought experience.' There is, in the Bible, a dual attitude towards the past. Paul bids us forget that which lies behind, and press on to the future in Christ, but again and again we are bidden with equal authority to consider God's dealing in past days, and build upon the foundations there laid.

It was part of Joshua's strength that he understood these obligations. It is the way of small, weak men to try to destroy the work of those who went before, as though their achievement provoked some invidious comparison with their own doings. Men of moral strength and confidence make every endeavour to weave what others have done into the texture of their own performance.

Joshua must have been mightily conscious of the fact that he captained a new movement of history. The Jordan river was a frontier in time as well as in place. He might easily have been tempted, like those who are unhealthily conscious of a rift called the 'generation gap', to work on entirely new principles, to carve a new path, with new attitudes, new ways. Instead of such damaging folly, he knew that the moral laws on which the present and the future depended had been grasped, applied, and written on tablets of enduring stone in Moses' day.

Hence his action after the next forward movement in the conquest of Canaan. He reaffirmed (30–35) the great principles on which Moses had worked. In a stage-setting deliberately evocative of the past, and recalling the very situation of a great challenge of his predecessor, Joshua reinstituted the ceremony of the blessings and the cursings. He revived and reiterated (35) the lawgiver's words, to the last syllable. It was an act of greatness. Israel was always conscious of its history, and built much hope, much courage, much endeavour upon the knowledge and understanding of it. Joshua set such a course when he took over the work of one of the greatest figures of all time and sought to construct his own contribution upon its solid base.

## 39 : Adonizedek

### Joshua 10

We are tracing in these studies the character and personality of men and women. Hundreds of human beings move through the pages of the Bible for good or for ill. Their words and deeds are woven with the message of the book to teach us what lessons they may. It will be a good practice for those who follow these notes to read the story as a continuous whole, though the specific reading may be only one portion.

In this chapter the person of a Canaanitish chief is chosen as typical of the whole group. This part of Joshua's story is grim reading. The words mingle with the clash of sword and spear, and the reek of burning villages. Adonizedek was one of the small feudal rulers of Palestine who had played his part, like the other petty despots of the land, in spreading the corruption and sanguinary religion which the flood of the Hebrew conquest swept away. It was a day of reckoning.

The land was 'defiled under its inhabitants' (cf. Isa. **24**.5), and the men who held authority in town and countryside were morally responsible for the blood and sadism, the cultic murder of infants, and all the other horrors of corrupt humanity which soiled the clean earth. The calamity which befell the 'kings' of Canaan must be judged in the light of these historic facts.

The story is briefly told. Much would be clearer were more

words available. Consider the case of another ruler of similar name, Adonibezek, whose story is told with one revealing detail in the first seven verses of the story of the judges (Judg. 1.1–7). The incident happens to record the sombre cruelty of the man which found just retribution at the hands of the Israelites. Cruelty shows utter corruption, and the archaeological evidence from the little towns of Canaan reveals the nature of the communities which the kings who meet their end in this chapter ruled over.

It is a principle of human history that men and nations reap what they sow. It is certain enough that the solid retribution which fell upon the defeated enemies of Joshua was nothing more than the dark harvest of their own deeds. Joshua must not therefore, as Israel's ruler, be regarded as a stony monumental figure, hard and merciless, but a man hot with anger at evil, and deeply conscious that he cleansed a land. The 'iniquity of the Amorites' (Gen. 15.16) was at last full.


## 40 : Joshua's Success

### Joshua 11

Joshua had been promised success (1.8) and the conditions of winning it had been laid down. He had fulfilled the conditions completely, as the closing verses of ch. 10 show. He had obeyed the law. It was a terrible task, that of leading Israel to victory in the land, but as a soldier and administrator he served his country well.

It is appropriate here to mention a factor in that success. 'A successful man,' said Albert Einstein, 'is he who receives a great deal from his fellow men, usually incomparably more than corresponds to his service to them.' This is not always true. Joshua gave himself. He always had given himself without thought of personal advantage. He had provided leadership, and, by his faithfulness, an indispensable link with the past. The great scientist's remark, however, does touch one point of truth. Israel's multitude had played its part in the making of history.

A host of unnamed men and women were a part of the history of these years. They move dimly through the murk and the noise which fill these chapters, but bravery, endurance and readiness to follow and obey must have been common marks of the men and women of the Hebrew host. We glimpse them in the long march round Jericho, circling the little fortress by the Jordan, and perhaps not understanding the purpose of what seemed an aimless manoeuvre. They maintained the ban of silence imposed upon them under the invective from the walls. Such were the people who backed Joshua's success and made it possible.

Those who are led reflect the qualities of the leader. A riotous and undisciplined army is an indication of undisciplined weakness in the man at the head. An ordered, self-controlled host, is a sure reflection of the stern and sturdy character of the leader. The nature of authority inevitably filters down and shows itself in the morale of the organization which that authority controls or fails to control. Joshua had his success. He owed it to his nation, but his nation had equal debt to him. 'Nothing fails like success,' someone has said. Joshua bore success with dignity. He knew to whom he owed it and it never tempted him to arrogance or to self-esteem. He had learned Moses' lessons well. It was all 'by faith'.

## 41 : Caleb

### Joshua 14

We are permitted to meet one of the multitude who contributed to the triumph of Joshua. Caleb appears again in the next chapter and briefly in Judg. 1. It is good to meet the old man again. 'An old man's past's a strange thing,' said John Masefield, 'for it never leaves his mind.' Not so with Caleb. He can, to be sure, speak of the brave days when he served Moses, but he is forward-looking, eager to accomplish something more before the end. Writing his famous essay on old age, at the age of 63, Cicero remarked: 'As I approve of the youth who has something of the old man in him, so I am no less pleased with the old man that has something of the youth. He that follows this rule may be old in body but can never be so in mind.' Tennyson touched the same theme in his magnificent *Ulysses*:

*How dull it is to pause and make an end,*
*To rust unburnish'd, not to shine in use!*
*As though to breathe were life . . .*

. . . . . . . . . .

*Old age hath yet his honour and his toil.*

. . . . . . . . . .

*Tho' much is taken, much abides; and tho'*
*We are not now that strength which in old days*
*Moved earth and heaven; that which we are, we are;*
*One equal temper of heroic hearts,*
*Made weak by time and fate, but strong in will*
*To strive, to seek, to find, and not to yield.*

Caleb would have agreed. He is among the valiant old men of the Bible—Barzillai, Simeon, John, are others—and he sets the tone; 'and not to yield'. Clement Attlee quoted those words in tribute to Winston Churchill, and it is difficult to imagine a better motto as the years pile up behind . . . 'We shall never surrender.'

But the time arrives for certain resolutions. Unyieldingness should not hold the old man to tasks another can do better. He must learn gracefully to retire before he irks and burdens those whose respect he wishes to retain. He must learn to listen more and talk less, to avoid the temptation of capping every tale. Above all, let the future remain a challenge, as Caleb found it, a time to claim the unclaimed promise, to finish the unfinished task. Said Ulysses:

*Vile it were to store and hoard myself,*
*With this grey spirit yearning in desire*
*To follow Knowledge like a sinking star . . .*

There is still a path to tread. John wrote his Gospel in his nineties.

## 42 : Phinehas

### Joshua 22

Said John Foster Dulles once: 'When the world thermometer registers "not war, not peace" it is hard to decide whether to follow military or political judgements.' It is perhaps easier to follow spiritual judgements, and to do that requires a diplomat of deep understanding and insight. In Phinehas we meet such a man. He cuts a fine figure.

There was a real danger lest the Jordan should become a divisive frontier through the very body of Israel. The twisting river is no great military obstacle, but it easily becomes a line in the minds of men, and there was some peril lest the tribes which had petitioned for a portion on the desert side of Jordan should become dissociated from those who occupied the land west of the river, Israel's heart-land.

It was obvious that the faith which Abraham had brought from Ur of the Chaldees, and the Law which Moses had given as the form and organization of that faith, were the cement which held the tribes of Israel together. When the trans-Jordanian segments set up their altar, it appeared that division, and the sundering of a hard-won unity, was on the way. It was to come thus in later centuries.

Phinehas was the very man for the task of protest and investigation. He speaks with frankness, but a frankness seasoned with tact and courtesy. He delivers his warning faithfully, with appeal to historic precedents. He approaches those to whom he was sent with dignity and clarity of speech. Of an ambassador no one can expect more.

Hence, in chief measure, his success. The language of the reply reflects the language of the protest and the appeal—courteous, earnest, sincere. Their altar, they said, was not schismatic and in no sense intended to replace the altar which symbolized the unity of Israel. It was a mere memorial cairn, designed, not to divide, but to recall a unity which Jordan might have challenged.

Phinehas was no man of war. He came to his task cool, open-minded, ready to believe the best. An ambassador must be a man of peace, and lay hold of peace, if peace may be had on terms of honour. This was the peace which Phinehas brought back from across the great Rift Valley. It is a reflection of his worth and his wisdom, no less than of his eloquence.

# 43 : Joshua's Charge

## Joshua 23.1—24.28

Joshua saw his final task in a brave reminder. The old see more truly the significance of history because they see the meaning of their own life's experience. With rugged courage he faced the people with their past. Man was man even in that ancient century, and the 'generation gap' was no doubt apparent and exaggerated. Those were rising who knew nothing of the blood and toil, and sweat and tears, which had bought the good they knew and the peace they now enjoyed.

Each generation must choose, because although the past has its dire lessons as well as its inspiration and encouragement, it is fatal to live in the past. Paul himself is witness to that (Phil. **3**.13), and the experience of the first disciples (John **6**.66). An equal list of Scripture texts could support the other lessons, that the past is neglected to our peril. A balanced life is lived if all the experience of the years that lie behind is interwoven with the needs, the movements and the tasks of the present.

And the choice, man's age-old choice, is between God and whatever stands against Him, be it the base heritage of Canaan, or Baal, or Antichrist. They ever tug, and the pull of the society in which we live is a tension to resolve. Paul wrote: 'I therefore implore you, brothers, in the name of God's mercies, to dedicate your bodies as a living sacrifice, consecrated to God, well-pleasing to Him, which is the worship proper to your nature. *And cease trying to adapt yourself to the age you live in, but continue your transformation by the renewing of your mind,* to the end that you may test out for yourselves the will of God, that, namely, which is good, well-pleasing to him, and perfect' (Rom. **12**.1 f. E.M.B.).

Note the closing words of **24**.15. The old man made no oratorical pause. There was no quick look to see which way the crowd was moving, no attempt to assess the mood of the people and adapt his words thereto. He was not a leader of that sort. He took his stand, and he took it for his house. It is a notable fact that this is what produced the response of the people (16).

Joshua tested them further. Perhaps some unrecorded event of national backsliding lies behind the hard words of v. 19.

Joshua took and bound them by a ritual act, especially sacred in that Eastern context. Brief, pungent, unyielding and without a syllable of compromise, he fixed their decision firmly in their minds.

## 44 : Joshua's Passing

### Joshua 24.29–33; Judges 2.1–10

Here are two more lines to add to the quotation (Study 40) from Tennyson's *Ulysses* . . . They could have been written of Joshua :

> *Death closes and all: but something ere the end*
> *Some work of noble note may yet be done . . .*

How true indeed of the son of Nun. He had watched the green old age of Moses, perhaps, too, the last vigour of the unrecorded Nun. He had seen Caleb strong and valiant in his closing days. And now death was creeping also on him. He had not the clear view out beyond death which is the Christian's glorious privilege, though he no doubt took it for granted, as all ancient peoples did, that the grave was not the final terminus, life's utter end.

How a man faces the last enemy, tells much of his character through life. It matters 'how we all go out at journey's end'. And that last phrase was first coined by Dryden :

> *With equal mind what happens let us bear,*
> *Nor joy nor grieve too much for things beyond*
> *our care,*
> *Like pilgrims to th'appointed place we tend;*
> *The world's an inn and death the journey's end.*

Resolution, dignity, care for those yet to be, valiant example, words of ripe wisdom—these all showed the man. That some heard him, and carried the banner on, is demonstrated by the fact that another generation stood true after his passing (**2**.10). Youth thinks the end remote, and life an endless journey. Life hurries on, appearing to accelerate with the years. It is a good and healthful thing to look at those who march to the boundary, like Joshua, unsoiled. There is jubilation in ending well. Said Saul Kane in Masefield's poem:

> *I wondered then why life should be,*
> *And what would be the end of me*
> *When youth and health and strength were gone*
> *And cold old age came creeping on.*

No need to wonder for those who hold fast to Christ, and watch men like Joshua—or Paul. For those who seek a New Testament reading turn now to the last words of the great apostle to the Gentiles which close the second of the two letters to young Timothy.


## Questions and themes for study and discussion on Studies 38–44

1. The differing roles of tradition and creativity in the work of a leader.
2. The unnamed men and women of the Bible.
3. What are the prime qualities of good leadership?
4. What are the chief tasks of old age?
5. What are the dangers of diplomacy?
6. What is the finest service of old age?

# THE CHARACTER OF GOD

## A Holy and Righteous God
## (c) Displayed in Gospel and Epistle

### 45 : God's Judgement, Present and Future

#### Matthew 3

In studying the passages that follow, we must notice whether the New Testament modifies the Old Testament revelation of God as holy and righteous. Today's chapter is an interim between the two Testaments, John the Baptist being the final prophet of the Old and the usherer in of the New (1 ff., cf. Matt. 11.11–14).

The coming of the Messianic King, here identified with Jehovah (3, Isa. 40.3), means the introduction of the Kingdom (2), even though it is not yet set up in all its visible glory. Many thought that the Messiah would automatically deliver the nation from the domination of Rome, but John asserts that the Kingdom involves personal repentance and coming to terms with the King. The primary enemies were not the Romans, but themselves (cf. 1.21). We have read of those who treated the Temple as a charm (Jer. 7.4); here we have them trusting in their descent from Abraham (9). John's words in v. 9 foreshadow Gal. 3.28 f.

John's baptism required repentance, and, by implication, faith that the Messiah was about to come. Christian baptism involves repentance, and faith in the Messiah who has indeed come and brought salvation (Acts 2.38; 19.1–6). Judgement and salvation are opposite sides of the coin; if wheat is gathered in, chaff is burnt (12). This is not simply the opinion of an embittered prophet, but is the same picture as Jesus Christ Himself used (e.g. Matt. **13**.30, 41–43). It is in fact a reassertion of all that we have studied in the Old Testament.

What is the significance of 'the Holy Spirit and *with fire*'? Is this the fire of judgement, the alternative to the Spirit's work (12)? Or is it Pentecost (Acts **2**.3), the only occasion in the New Testament where fire symbolizes anything other than destruction or testing? We need not draw a hard line between the two possibilities. The Holy Spirit purifies as well as empowers (e.g. Rom. **8**.1–11), and fire refines as well as destroys (e.g. 1 Cor. **3**.13–15; 1 Pet. **1**.7).

John is truly humble (11, 14). He realizes that he is face to face with One who had no sin and who therefore need not undergo the baptism of repentance (14). The reply of Jesus showed that He wished for the other aspect of the baptism, as committal to the righteous standards of the Kingdom (15). Since as King He was inaugurating this fresh stage in the coming of the Kingdom, His baptism became the occasion for His designation as Son of God in the Messianic sense (16 f.; Psa. **2**.7, cf. John **1**.32–34), although He was Son of God from the moment of conception (Luke **1**.31–35), and, indeed, from eternity.

*Compare what is said of John as God's representative in Luke* 1.67–79.


## 46 : God's Work from Within

### Luke 11.37–53

In this searching passage we again meet the familiar reference to externals and internals (37–41). There is everything to be said for generous giving, but let this come as the spontaneous God-implanted desire of the heart, and not as a substitute bribe to God or a display to man (41).

Scrupulosity over details can cover a lack of care for fundamental morality and love for God (42). To be known as a Pharisee was to shine before the people. Pomp and display may impress (43), but what standards do people find to follow in those who impress them? When the inner values of leaders do not reflect God, they lower the values of their followers (44, cf. Matt. **23**.27).

The lawyers (45) were the same as the scribes. They interpreted the written revelation. Down the ages the interpretations became more and more intricate, and at times contradicted the original revelation and gave a totally distorted view of God (e.g. Mark **7**.9–13). The intricacies of legalism were blinding leaders and people to the straightforward message of Jesus Christ (46, 52). Thus the leaders were in the line of their forefathers, who persecuted the prophets when they rebuked them for choosing externals at the expense of truth of heart (47 f.).

Just as Jeremiah and Ezekiel saw the end of an era as God's judgement on unholiness and unrighteousness, so Christ now warned of an accumulated judgement that would come on the generation that had completely failed to learn from the past, and so were about to reject the One who was greater than any of the prophets. God's hand in the past should be an important teacher.

We know from rabbinic writings that there were good Pharisees who were not content with externals, and the New Testament gives favourable mention to Nicodemus, Joseph of Arimathea, and Gamaliel (Acts **5**.34). But the general methods of Pharisees, Sadducees, and their Scribes led to the evils of which Christ spoke, and to the rejection of the sinless Messiah as an agent of Satan (Matt. **10**.25; **12**.24). Yet one may wonder how far Pharisaism in the churches would reject Christ if He came as a Man on earth again.

*What does the New Testament teach about inner renewal if we are to be like God?*

## 47 : The Rejection of God in Christ

### Luke 20.1–18

During the last few days before the crucifixion, Jesus Christ had a final confrontation with the religious leaders of the nation. This was no private discussion. As happened often with the prophets (e.g. Jer. **26**.2), it was a public challenge before crowds of spectators who were sufficiently concerned to come up to Jerusalem for the festival. These were the people who shortly afterwards would have to give their verdict for Jesus or Barabbas.

At the moment the crowd were evidently on the side of Jesus, as vs. 1–8 indicate. Although John the Baptist had not conveyed authority to Jesus, most people knew that he had named Jesus as the Messiah. Thus Jesus was not quibbling when He asked His alternative question. The sin of the leaders was the failure to look at the evidence seriously, since, if John and Jesus were truly commissioned by God, their own attitude would be radically shaken. The genuine conversion of religious leaders on any point is hard for them to face. Their refusal to answer shows their fear of facing the evidence.

In vs. 9–18 Christ, as in the previous portion, links the present with the past. If the leaders would not face contemporary evidence, they were equally slow to learn lessons from the nation's history. God's tenants have manipulated His vineyard in their own interest, and have not handed over any fruit when prophet-messengers came to look for it. So God sends His Son, and it is significant that Christ distinguishes Himself as in a different category from the prophets and other godly men (13 f.). God has acted in mercy and is offering the present tenants the chance to redeem the past, but the murder of His Son makes their final break with Him. Now, as once or twice before in history, God will act in physical judgement. The vineyard must have a fresh start under new tenants (16).

So it is to be opened to Gentile, as well as Jewish, tenants. Although the Son of God was crucified, His death can still be for life as well as for judgement. To change the picture, the religious leaders would not build on Him, but despite this He would become the cornerstone of the new living Temple (Eph. 2.20–22). The context here is naturally weighted on the side of judgement, and Jesus Christ, once rejected by the builders, is still a stone that decides the destiny of individuals.

*Study the references to God's Stone in Psa. 118.22 f.; Isa. 8.14 f.; 28.16 f.; Zech. 3.9; 4.7; Acts 4.11; Rom. 9.32 f.; Eph. 2.19–21; 1 Pet. 2.4–8.*

## 48 : Open to God and Man

### Acts 5.1–16

The story of Ananias and Sapphira stands near to the beginning of the history of the early Church as Achan's story stands at the entrance of the chosen people to the promised land (Josh. 7). It is a reminder that, even though God does not intervene obviously on every occasion of personal or national sin, He has imprinted His judgement on certain historical events for us to ponder in our reading.

The sin of Ananias and Sapphira has often been repeated in one way or another. Hypocrisy may deceive men, but not God. The early Church was not governed by a compulsory communism, but by God-inspired generosity and care (4.34). Ananias and Sapphira could have contributed as much or as little as they felt they could afford (4), but their sin lay in not being open, but rather in professing to have given all the proceeds of the sale to the relief funds (2, 8), just as Achan professed to have kept nothing for himself from the spoils of Jericho.

We are not obliged to draw a hard line between natural and supernatural in the deaths of this husband and wife. If they died through guilty fear, it was fear of God (9) and not of Peter; yet it is also true that God inflicted the judgement of sudden death upon them. In stories like this we can see the ultimate admission by human beings of the holiness and righteousness of God.

The remaining verses (12–16) show a magnificent work that might have been blocked if there had been others like Ananias and Sapphira in the Church. At this point the judgement that Christ foretold had not fallen on the nation. The crucified Messiah was now the risen Messiah, and the way was open for leaders and people to turn to Him. But the leaders were among 'the rest' (13), and would not come in as one-by-one believers, as so many ordinary people were coming, in spite of the demonstration that God was behind the Christians (15 f.).

*Is hypocrisy a sin against God or man?*

# 49 : A Lost Eternity

## 2 Thessalonians 1

By considering God as holy and righteous, we have seen that unholiness and unrighteousness inevitably separate from Him. The Old Testament, with only a small amount of revelation about the future life, has shown us God's work in nature and grace to bring man back to Himself here and now. His response to perpetuated sin is not bad temper, but wrath. This is an emotive word to describe His inevitable rejection of evil, and, since evil is not an abstract substance, of the person who has absorbed the evil. We can accept this, and still say that God loves the sinner but hates his sin. The Bible, by showing God's acts of redemption, demonstrates this, since, if He did not love the sinner, God would not work to bring him back to Himself, and, if He did not hate the sin, He would have no need to provide redemption from the sin.

This present chapter takes us from here-and-now into eternity. Peace with God, and the experience of His power to save and make whole, must begin in this life (2–4, 10–12). If not, and if a person goes into eternity cut off from God, there is no hint in the New Testament that this state of separation will ever end (8 f.). Having built up a self-sufficient personality that is excluded from peace with God and the enjoyment of His presence, it would seem that the renewal of this personality is impossible once this world is left behind. Ruin and exclusion are the natural and supernatural outcome (9).

If the Bible gives no hint of a reversal after death (note Luke 16.26) or of universalism, none of us is called upon to judge how many have never had a first chance and would have accepted Christ if they had. What we do know is that we are charged to take the gospel to all the world, and not rest our hopes on some sort of salvation for the heathen through default.

Those to whom Paul refers here are primarily those who, when faced with the gospel and the demonstrated power of God, choose to persecute rather than to come to the knowledge of God themselves (6–8). They experience the vengeance of God (8), though, since this word may carry overtones of an unfair violent outburst, we may prefer the translation 'to impose the penalty' (Jer. Bible) or 'do justice upon' (NEB).

*Consider the gain and loss in this chapter.*


## 50 : Presuming on God

### Hebrews 10.26–39

The previous portion was concerned with obvious unbelievers. Now we have those who at least have made a Christian profession, even though they have now gone back on it. Commentators differ over whether it was anything more than a profession. In this brief note we must simply take the practical facts. The New Testament speaks of eternal safety for those who are Christ's (e.g. John 10.28 f.). We are not dropping in and out of salvation all the time. There are, however, some warnings, so that we cannot say, 'Now that I am saved, it does not matter what I do.'

This passage and Heb. 6.1–12 are two such warnings. Clearly they do not refer to some isolated sin, but to an attitude. Equally certainly, they cannot mean that no backslider can ever be restored. The emphasis in both places is upon rejection of Christ and His death. Such rejection may begin practically by choosing something from which we have been redeemed, and may then be supported by spurious theology (cf. Rom. 6.1 f.). Note the present tense in the Greek of 6.6; i.e. 'since they are crucifying' (NEB), or even, 'while they are crucifying'. So in 10.26 there is no longer any alternative way of forgiveness if the sacrifice of Christ is deliberately spurned, whether practically or theologically (29), since once again one stands naked before the judgement of God. If God were an idol, with whom fellowship was impossible, this would not matter; but we have no defence if we spurn the God who is life and who gives life (31).

Answers for Christian living are in the verses that follow. (*a*) Remember past struggles (32–34). It is easy to relax once the first emotions of conversion have died down. (*b*) Let the view of God's eternity overshadow the material present (34 f., cf. 11.13–16). (*c*) Much of the Christian life involves steady patience rather than a series of sudden uplifts (36). (*d*) Remember our accountability at the judgement seat of Christ when He returns (37). (*e*) Faith and righteousness are welded together in Scripture, and our lives must demonstrate this (38 f.).

*Compare what this passage says about God-centred faith and endurance with Phil. 3.*

## 51 : The Life of God-likeness

### 1 Peter 1.13–25

This portion rounds off all that we have been studying about God as holy and righteous. It contains the key passage which links divine and human holiness together (15 f.), and which, as a quotation from Lev. 11.44 f., also links the two Testaments. As God's revelation has unfolded, His nature and character have become clearer, and consequently we have been shown more and more of what it means to be like God. If we say that likeness to God is salvation, we can see the Bible presentation of salvation as something more than being pulled into heaven when we die.

We have been saved by grace, but the final work of grace will come when Christ is revealed at His Second Coming (13). Experience shows that holiness in this life is not absolute perfection, but in addition to the final grace there is also the day-by-day efficacy of the blood of Jesus Christ (19, cf. 1 John 1.7).

Meanwhile we have the possibility of like-God holiness, since God Himself has called us (15) as responsible and accountable beings (17), and has bought us out of our un-reconciled state through the sacrificial death of the Lord Jesus Christ (18 f.). His forgiveness is not grounded on a mental picture or on myth, but on solid historical fact (20), which gives objective reality for faith (21). In responding to the guaranteed message of the gospel, we have been born anew as children of God (22–25), to experience 'Like Father, like son (or daughter)'.

Yet we are members of two worlds, and there are habit tracks that would pull us back to the old (14) if our way is not deliberately set on the practical likeness to God that shows itself by being 'mentally stripped for action, perfectly self-controlled' (13, Jer. Bible), and showing love from the heart (22).

*Consider vs. 20 f., as anchor verses for the Christian.*

## Questions and themes for study and discussion on Studies 45–51

1. What do these passages (and others if you wish) teach about Christian accountability to God?
2. How can accountability to God be reconciled with salvation through grace?
3. How far is the essential nature of hell (as e.g. in 2 Thes. 1.9) an extension of the state of the lost in this life? Is C. S. Lewis justified in his allegory *The Great Divorce,* when he pictures the lost being allowed into heaven and then choosing to return to hell?
4. To what extent does Pharisaism exist today among (i) believers, (ii) non-believers, and how far is it a genuine misunderstanding of the nature of God?

# CHARACTER STUDIES

## 52 : The Judges

### Judges 1—3

The theme passes with the next book of the Old Testament into a sombre period of history, a time when 'startled faces flicker in the gloom', and the plan of God for His people became a mere rill in the wilderness of history.

It was an age of battle and of violence. Consider Othniel, Ehud and Shamgar of these early chapters. 'War,' wrote Thucydides in one of the most penetrating chapters of Greek history, 'is a rough schoolmaster, and brings most men's characters to the level of their fortunes.' This was true of these grim years.

Moses was gone. Joshua was gone. Israel lacked a great leader. The men who rose to deliver and to guide, and moments of crisis seemed to bring them to the fore, were lesser men, with some rudiments of faith in God, but little insight into the character of God, to ennoble and to soften them. These strong and sometimes brutal men were called 'saviours' (3.9, 15), more because of the opportuneness of their leadership than its quality.

It was, in fact, a 'dark age' for Israel, with wide disorganization, tribal discord and defeat. To see in the judges who successively rose and ruled, from Othniel to Samson, a 'type of Christ' (in anything but their mere office), as one commentator puts it, is to distort exegesis beyond recognition. As the words of Thucydides, the Greek historian, had it in the above quotation, the times produced the men, and few could see in the treacherous Ehud, for all the political advantage of the murder he committed, much resembling Christ in actuality or symbol.

This is not to deny in any way that God overruled in such troubled times, but it is a principle of God's action in history that He works through such men as seek Him, and that quest is sometimes a fumbling and a groping in the dark by ignorant and confused people who know little of His ways. This is the lesson we shall have occasion again and again to learn as we read this sad book, and meet its primitive characters. Passion and determination they had. Witness Shamgar with his crude armament. Of these early three judges there is no mention of faith, goodness, or those great qualities we found in Moses and Joshua, and many of the men who caught their bright reflection. But 'God was in the shadows keeping watch upon His own'.


## 53 : Deborah and Barak

### Judges 4, 5

It is strange, yet logical, to take these two persons together. Deborah is the most sharply drawn character we have so far met in the book. Barak is a mere shadow beside her, and one suspects some weakness and timidity in the man (4.8). There are those who are born to follow, but sometimes those who accept such a lowly role when higher honour beckons, lose in reputation what they gain in effectiveness, as Deborah warned her captain of the northern host (4.9). But she in no way despised him.

It was, to be sure, a perilous and terrifying situation. Hazor was a major stronghold, a Canaanitish city which had taken full advantage of the Iron Age, whose techniques were developing. And furthermore the Esdraelon plain was ideal terrain for armoured warfare. Sisera had 900 chariots, and it was the intervention of the flash-flood and vicious rain-storm (5.20 f.) which gave the ill-armed Israelitish tribesmen the victory. But we miss in Barak the dash and resolution with which true leaders of men face overwhelming odds. In the social context of that day it was shame to accept the leadership of a woman however able she had proved herself to be.

Of that ability there is no doubt. It was perhaps 1125 B.C. Deborah was a prophetess in the most ancient significance of that word. She was of great and recognized wisdom (4.4–8), and used her insight and understanding to dispense justice from a primitive court held under a palm tree which became an historic monument (4.5). To gain such acceptance among the rough tribesmen, distracted in their feuds, and amid the social disorganization of this early day, betokened a woman of great and noble character and charm. Observe that Barak obeys her swift, decisive commands, and that he claims the advantage of her presence because of the aura which surrounded her person as well as because of a certain hesitation, born of the timidity within him, to seize and hold the part which the prophetess was eager to grant him. Her willingness to send Barak on the campaign as sole commander, itself throws some light on Deborah's quality. There was no laying hold of authority, beyond that willingly ceded by her people, in her. Oddly enough, Hebrews 11.32 mentions only Barak among the heroes of faith.

## 54 : Deborah's Song

### Judges 5

The songs sung by an age or a people teach much about the society from which they spring. So do the songs of men and women in the context of their personal experience. We have the song of Miriam (Exod. 15.21), but that was a response to the psalm of Moses, who was a lyrist in his own right.

Deborah's song is the song of a triumphant woman, to be set beside the psalms of women recorded by Luke in the early chapters of his Gospel. Historically it has its significance, for it teaches something of the relations between the tribes in the far twelfth century before Christ. It is also a source of information about the events at hand. Only from the song do we hear of the natural causes which frustrated Sisera and placed opportunity in Barak's hands, the flash-flood and the swollen Kishon.

Deborah, the authoress, is vividly evident in the words. She sounds a note of genuine praise to God, and from such allegiance flows her social conscience. She passes rapidly from the thought of God's providence to the conception of peace, justice and class harmony, which necessarily flow from such a faith and gratitude so real. She found a unity based in history, and the malediction on Meroz (5.23), the town which broke that unity in the day of stress, whips harshly into the paean of praise. Here was the stern side of Israel's Joan of Arc. Without that side to her character she could not have served such a day.

The same facet of character is shown in the praise of Jael, who killed Sisera. It was an act of war, and as such was accepted by the warrior-prophetess. 'A note of sympathy,' characteristic of a woman, says one commentator, is evident in the little vignette of Sisera's mother, looking out for her son's returning. It is difficult, however, to see anything in these grimly jubilant verses (28–30) of softness or sympathy. Deborah triumphs over the alien woman, and the gloating over Israel's spoil which the poem rightly imagines on the foreigner's lips, leaves little room to lament the bereavement she suffered, when Hazor's Guderian failed to reach his home. Upon the invader fell the retribution of the Law, and we have met a fierce, loyal and able woman of the Law.


## 55 : Gideon

### Judges 6.1–27

Between the lines of Gideon's story may be read again the plight of Israel, their precarious tenure of the land, and their vulnerability to their foes. The Amalekites and the Midianites were tribes of desert nomads, Bedouin of sorts, who haunted the eastern borderlands, where the desert impinges on 'the sown'. Gideon's secret threshing of the wheat (11) reveals the helplessness of the people against the raiding from the wilderness. It was high time for a new leader, and Gideon, of all the men who have moved through the story since the death of Joshua, was most fitted for the role.

Observe that Hebrews (11.32) lists Gideon among the heroes of faith, but it is significant that the story itself stresses the caution and tentative approach which inhibited faith in the hero. It is not triumphant confidence alone which is honoured of God. He rewards 'the grain of mustard seed'. It is clear that Gideon was a harassed and discouraged man. He bore the burdens of long defeat. He was unaided by any strong surviving tradition. When the messenger of God first summoned him to the task of national deliverance, it was with bitter unbelief that he at first responded (13). The only explanation he found to offer for the sorry state of his nation was that God, who had once been at hand with present aid, had forsaken His people.

'And the Lord looked upon him' (14, AV[KJV]), says the text, and evidently saw more within him than the words upon his lips could show. It is not always possible to judge a man from what he says, and the penetrating glance of deeper understanding revealed in Gideon the reality of belief which could be used.

Note now two turns in the story. Gideon asked for confirmation. He was to do it again in the matter of the fleece and the dew. It is an indication of his character—a deep dislike of rash and hasty action. It is not always possible, indeed it is seldom right and good, to importune God for proof. Sometimes, however, divine grace meets us at the place and point of our feeble faith, and grants a demonstration of God's reality. Gideon had his demonstration (21).

Secondly, he was bidden himself to demonstrate his faith by works. It was essential for a man so cautious to commit himself, and to turn belief into salutary action. Gideon required no small courage to go forth against the apostate cults which were beginning to infiltrate the borderlands of Israel. Deliverance began as deliverance does by a cleansing act and a movement of consecration.

## 56 : Joash

### Judges 6.28–32

Gideon had asked for signs. If his eyes were open to the movements of God's hand, he had a sign indeed in the loyalty of his own father. Brave old Joash moves into the story on the morrow of his son's idol-breaking. There are parents whose examples bring a son to a knowledge of God. In rarer instances the stream flows backward and a son is salvation to his father.

Joash is good to meet. No sooner had he seen the decisiveness of his son's action than he recognized its rectitude, and moved to his defence. Perhaps he had himself known long since what should have been done, but had hesitated to act. Now the deed was done, and, late though the hour was, Joash took his stand. Perhaps we can add a verse to Marianne Farningham's variation of Charlotte Elliott's well-known evangelistic hymn.

> *Just as I am, though youth is past,*
> *And the leaves grow brown in the autumn blast,*
> *Though few be the years I can give—at last,*
> *Lord of all life, I come.*

The appearance of Joash is brief but effective. He must have been one who had won the respect of his fellow villagers of Ophrah. It is no light matter to face a hostile crowd. Feelings ran high and violence was in the air when the old man stepped forward to address the crowd. They had lost their god—so be it—was he not the sun-god, and was his blazing sign not a witness to the scene, high in the heaven? Cannot Baal look after himself? *Dis iniuriae dis curae,* says Tacitus— 'wrongs done to the gods are the gods' concern'. Something like that is intended in the new name Joash gives now to his son. It is a taunt given in irony against Baal-worship, if its meaning is: 'Let Baal fight against him' (C. F. Kraft in the *Interpreter's Dictionary of the Bible.*)

The Hebrew peasantry were simple hard-headed men, and the plain common sense of Joash's argument seems to have appealed to them. The old man had something of Elijah in him, for the challenge in the name of Jerubaal was in the same spirit as Elijah's taunts on Carmel, three centuries later. The story of Joash is brief, and hardly rounded-off in the fast-moving narrative, but the end is clear. The people listened and Gideon survived to save them.


## 57 : Gideon's Testing

### Judges 6.33–7.7

The Midianites were in the Esdraelon Plain, otherwise Jezreel, ideal terrain for armoured war like that of Sisera, but not the type of country for camel-borne Bedouin. Gideon, however, could see the extent of the twin forces from the hills, and took the precaution of calling a general rally. There was nothing wrong in this, but the tribal forces of Israel were not in a condition to fight. Gideon may have observed the signs of disorder, apprehension, lack of spirit and assurance. It was discouraging.

Hence his yearning for a 'sign', always a mark of feeble faith. The dew on the fleece was a not unnatural phenomenon. In the Negev, the phenomenon of v. 38 can be repeated on any dewy morning. Hence the revival of ancient farming methods, and stone mulching in the area. Hence Gideon's timid request for confirmation.

Gideon has presumed to test God. God now tests him (7.2). Did Shakespeare have v. 3 in mind when he made Henry cry before the clash at Agincourt?—

> *Rather proclaim it, Westmoreland, through all my host,*
> *That he which hath no stomach to this fight,*
> *Let him depart; his passport shall be made,*
> *And crowns for convoy put into his purse.*

It is a sorry comment on the state of the land that over two-thirds of the host departed.

Now came the further test. Gideon was camped on the slopes of the hills. The rank and file were desperate with thirst, for the water lay at the foot where the riders of the raiding tribes could sweep down on watering-parties. The test seems to have been devised to separate the few who, in a moment of physical stress, set their duty of alertness in the face of the foe before the alleviation of their bodily need. Those who kept their eyes forward, and lifted the water in their hand, were the men Gideon needed.

All through the Bible God works by the few. Gideon needed this lesson. That he accepted it, and the ludicrous odds with which he faced the enemy, shows that his faith was growing. This is a principle of life. While we grow we live. Gideon was attaining the stature God desired in him.

## 58 : Gideon's Victory

### Judges 7.8—8.21

Gideon took his servant Purah to look more closely at the foe. God has tested him. He has faced the test. Now he is given some assurance. Add Purah to the list of worthy servants in the Bible. Some of them are well known—Joshua, for instance, and Timothy. Add those who are mere names, Jonathan's armourbearer, Elijah's servant, and others.

Gideon was not lacking in plain courage. It was an act of considerable daring to creep within hearing distance of the men in the nomad laager. The conversation thus overheard was of some significance. Wheat was grown on the fertile plain. Barley, the poorer crop, was grown on the less productive hill country. The barley loaf, which rolled destructively down into the camp of the Midianites, was a dream-symbol of a hillsmen's raid. It is a perfectly credible piece of psychology, the translation into phantasy of a genuine fear. Out of their proper element on the Jezreel Plain, the Midianites were afraid, and looking at the hills.

Gideon took intelligent advantage of the state of apprehension in which the invading tribesmen found themselves. He was a guerrilla leader of splendid resourcefulness, and his attack demonstrated what history has a hundred times revealed —that it is morale and confidence that matter, and that numbers are irrelevant. The coalition of the desert tribes was flung into confusion, and compelled to run the long and deadly gauntlet of the Jordan jungle and the trans-Jordan hill-country which separated them disastrously from the open desert which was their natural habitat. They were tangled in the land. Gideon had the victory.

'Reviewing the story of Gideon's life,' wrote Dr. Robert A. Watson, the leisurely Victorian commentator, 'we find this clear lesson, that within certain limits, he who trusts and obeys God has a quite irresistible efficiency.' This was his one lesson for Israel. The Mosaic law seems scarcely to have been known to him. But he did lay hold of God at the one point where his rudimentary faith could reach out and find Him—and God asks no more of any one of us . . . 'Yet,' Dr. Watson continues, 'seriously limited as he was, Gideon, when he had once laid hold of the fact that he was called by the unseen

God to deliver Israel, went on step by step to the great victory which made the tribes free.'

## 59 : Gideon at Peace

### Judges 8.22–28

Gideon was popular and, to his praise, rejected the temptation to found a royal dynasty on his popularity. This was greatly to his credit. We have noted earlier his touch of humility. It was one facet of the caution with which he moved towards the fulfilment of his call to lead Israel.

Surprisingly, that call seems to have evoked another sort of ambition. The Mosaic law, and the careful organization of the priesthood and the ritual of worship, were so obliterated in the common experience of Israel, that Gideon, having rejected royal estate, found the priesthood an acceptable aspiration. Weary of war, he desired holy office—an unexpected trait, and to be explained as a by-product of the deep experience of victory under God's hand which he had enjoyed in the Midian-Amalek war. 'A strong, but not spiritual religiousness,' writes the Victorian commentator, whom we have quoted, 'was the chief characteristic of Gideon's character.'

He was making a mistake. There are those who are drawn to the office of the priesthood or the ministry because of some glamour they imagine therein, or because of some personal search for peace, power or position. It was no doubt the first named, a quest for peace, that moved Gideon, but he had no right or calling in this desire.

His 'religiousness' made much of signs and symbols—the dew for example, and the sign of the angel. He now translates this into a form of action, and makes a rich ephod as a sign of his self-appointed office. This led, such is the desire of man for concrete objects of worship, to a new idolatry (27). The sign and symbol usurped the place of the reality.

And so Gideon died, a primitive figure of faith, little comprehending the wider issues of his day, but faithfully fulfilling the one task to which he was called. He gave his country peace, but beyond that he had nothing to give, and when his strong presence was gone, the land lapsed once more into the half-paganism which paralysed it.

1.  Why is Barak only and not Deborah mentioned in Heb. 11.32?
2.  'The hardest task that I can tell, is to play the second fiddle well.'
3.  Name six other great women of the Bible.
4.  Study a map of the Esdraelon plain and find the places mentioned in the story of Deborah and Barak. Where else do we meet the Kishon? Locate Carmel.
5.  What is faith?
6.  'The dearest idol I have known, whate'er that idol be. . . .' What are modern idols, and how can the problems they pose be tackled?

# THE CHARACTER OF GOD

## A Merciful and Compassionate God

A physiologist has to study parts of the human body in isolation, but remembers that the parts can be understood only in relation to the whole. We have been isolating the holiness and righteousness of God, and have seen Him in relation to His separation from sin, and also in relation to His removal of sin, so that we can be like Him in holiness. We can see how this latter aspect links on to the further revelation of His mercy and compassion, which we now begin to study somewhat in isolation.

## (a) Revealed in History and Psalm

### 60 : The Line of Divine Promise

#### Genesis 15

The choice of Abraham and his descendants was an act of compassion for the human race. Through them God would make Himself known as shield and reward (1), but above all as the One who reckons as righteous those who take Him at His word (6).

It was a regular custom for childless couples to adopt an heir, and Abraham had adopted the chief member of his household to inherit his property (2 f.). But God had not brought Abraham into the promised land for nothing. His own descendants would possess it (4, 5, 13–16), and clear it from Canaanite filth (16).

So God makes a covenant of promise. A Hebrew expression for making a covenant is 'cutting a covenant', and both parties sealed it by walking between a sacrifice that had been cut into two portions (10, 17; Jer. **34**.18 f.). So God as the initiator, and Abraham as the joint participant on behalf of all his descendants, form a covenant of mercy and compassion. Abraham's descendants include those who are the descendants of his justifying faith (Gal. **3**.6–9, 29).

The gift of the land as the incubation area of the promise was fulfilled in Solomon's time (1 Kings **4**.21, 24). Afterwards the superstitious clinging to the mere possession of the land, city and Temple (e.g. Jer. **7**.4), led to the gradual detachment of the promise from the land itself (cf. 1 Kings **9**.6–9), until in New Testament times, when Abraham's descendants were drawn from every nation, the promise was attached to the New Jerusalem which is above (Gal. **4**.26; Heb. **12**.22 f.).

*Study the application of v. 6 in Rom. **4** and Gal. **3**.*


## 61 : A Promise and a Prayer

### Genesis 18

Abraham had tried to secure the fulfilment of the promise of an heir (**15**.4) by having a son through Sarah's handmaid (**16**.1–4). This was an alternative to adoption in Abraham's day, and must have seemed to Abraham and Sarah the only way of obtaining God's promise now in view of their ages. But God had planned the best for them, setting His seal on the sanctity of monogamy.

So now He appears in human form, with two angels in attendance (1 f.). This is a fair interpretation in the light of the wording of vs. 1, 22, 33 and **19**.1. Although man could not see God in His absolute Being (John **1**.18), God occasionally assumed a form that could be observed by man's senses of sight, hearing, and touch.

The promise of a child for Sarah was the promise of a loving God, who, in spite of Sarah's panic, does not seem to have minded her surprised and delighted laughter (12–15). Would it be irreverent to say that He even teased her about it? So, at any rate, some have understood this passage.

Abraham is now taken further into the counsels of God. People of all nations were to claim his blessings for themselves (18), or were to be blessed in him (margin), so it is right that he should deliberate with God over mercy or judgement for the Gentile cities of Sodom and Gomorrah (17–21). While the angels go, the Lord remains (22).

Now follows one of the great God-inspired prayers of the Bible. We must see the prayer, not as though Abraham were more fair-minded than God, but as Abraham being permitted to take counsel with God. He stopped short when he came to ten righteous men (32), but he would have admitted that no one could ask for the cities to be spared if there were less than that. As it was, there were only four, Lot, his wife, and their two daughters, and the three latter had been contaminated by the standards of Sodom. Yet God in His mercy saved them by bringing them out from the doomed city.

*Consider this prayer as argument, acceptance, or mutual understanding.*


## 62 : Friend with Friend

### Exodus 33, 34

While Moses was absent on Sinai, the people made a golden calf and worshipped it as their god. Chapter 32 records how Moses dealt drastically with the sin, and yet interceded for the people.

Now God forces the people to realize what it would mean to try to occupy the promised land without His presence or under the threat of His judgement (1–3). As a sign of humble repentance, they strip themselves of their ornaments (4–6). The tent of v. 7 is not the Tabernacle, which was not yet made, and which was pitched in the centre of the camp. It may have been Moses' own tent at a time when he was the mediator between God and the people. Here God talked to him as Friend with friend (11). The position outside the camp emphasized the gap that sin had opened up, although the way of mediated communion was there for individuals who wished to come (7).

As friend with Friend Moses talks to God, as Abraham did (12 ff.). Moses was a genuinely humble man, aware of his own weaknesses (12, cf. 4.10). Now he asks for a vision of the Lord, a fuller understanding of His ways, and the assurance of His presence, which was unique to Israel (13–16).

So God promises a fresh revelation to sight and hearing of His glory and the gracious goodness of His character (19). Since no man can look on God in His fullness, Moses must be hidden by God's hand in a cleft rock (cf. 'Rock of Ages') until the glory has almost faded (21–23).

The vision was given on Sinai (34.1–4). A bright cloud partially hid the glory (5, cf. Matt. 17.5) as the Lord impressed His character on Moses in terms that would strike home to the nation's leader. The emphasis is on what Moses longed to hear—the mercy of God, His forbearance, and His steadfast covenant love (6 f.). Yet this is tempered, as Moses well knew, by the righteousness which could not clear those who, with their descendants, chose to remain in their sin (7).

Moses identifies himself with the nation, and asks for pardon and for the presence of the Lord (8 f.). God promises to take up His people again and demonstrate Himself in their history (10).

Since the incident of the golden calf had broken the Godward part of the covenant of chs. 20–24, God repeats and reinforces this (11–26), while leaving the social laws untouched.

Even the partial vision of the glory of God was absorbed into Moses' face (29). He had a foretaste of something that we too will experience through the mercy of God (Rev. 22.3–5).

*What does the New Testament say about our experience of the glory of God here and now? See, e.g. John 1.14–18; 2 Cor. 3.12–18.*


## 63 : Covenant Love

### Deuteronomy 7.6–26

There are two great covenant words in the Old Testament. One is SHALOM (both vowels long), regularly translated *peace.* The other is KHESED (both vowels short) which the AV (KJV) translates variously as *mercy, kindness, loving kindness, goodness.* The RSV almost always translates it as *steadfast love* (e.g. 9, 12). The NEB tries to keep the idea of covenant by such translations as *covenant and faith* (9), *keep faith* (12), and *loyalty* (Hos. **6**.6).

The close relation with *covenant* in vs. 9, 12 shows that it is not a casual word of general goodwill, but is the outgoing relationship that comes from a covenant bond. It is used almost always of God's attitude to man, but occasionally of man's response to God (e.g. Jer. **2**.2. *devotion*), and of man's attitude towards others who are bound by the same covenant (e.g. Hos. **6**.6).

In this portion, then, we study the Old Testament covenant as the expression of the steadfast love and compassion of God. The purpose of the covenant includes the expression of God's holiness to a world that does not know Him (6). The choice of Israel comes from the spontaneous love of God (7), but is itself grounded on the earlier promise to Abraham, Isaac, and Jacob (8). The demonstration of God's power is to be seen in the initial history of redemption from Egypt (8), in the direction of natural forces (13 f.), in health and strength (15), and in future history (16–24). All these outward demonstrations are what anyone would like to have. But God's power is also to be demonstrated in love and obedience from the heart (9–11), and in the people's ruthless cutting off of all that would entice away from God (16, 25 f.). We have already seen how the nation clamoured for the outward, and ignored the inward.

A noteworthy fact, in the light of Christian parallels, is the promise of gradual conquest (22). Often at conversion a number of enemies are swept right away, and cease to be temptations. Others remain, and only patient struggle will give victory. Some in the Philippian church thought they had jumped into total victory, but the beasts had crept in unobserved (Phil. **3**.12–19).

*Take this portion as a study in relationships with God and man.*

# 64 : God's Ways

## 1 Samuel 1.1—2.10

Several times in the Bible we read of God's choice of a child before he was born (e.g. Gen. **18**.9 ff.; Judg. **13**; Jer. **1**.5; Luke **1**.13 ff.; Gal. **1**.15). So here at a time of crisis God chose a mother for the last of the judges and the first of a line of prophets through whom He would continue to reveal Himself.

The emphasis here is on the unexpectedness of God's choice, and this is seized upon by Hannah in her meditation of thankfulness (**2**.1–10). Her experience, so trivial by the world's standards, is a reflection of far more spectacular acts of the Lord. He is holy (2). He is a strong defence (2). Because pride is unholy, and because the fancied strength of man is so often a God-substitute, God overthrows the proud and sets up the meek (3–5). Hannah remembers the taunts of her co-wife, who seemed to have everything (**1**.6). Her meditation takes in death and resurrection (6), and the entire reversal of human standards (7 f.). The Creator, who has built the world on firm foundations (8), cares for His people in the world, and will overthrow His opponents (9 f.).

Finally, the mother-to-be of the great prophet Samuel soars on the wings of inspired prophecy herself, and exults in the centring of all power and judgement in the Messianic king (10). This prayer is naturally compared with Mary's thanksgiving (Luke **1**.46–55) and the Beatitudes (Matt. **5**.3–12).

The actual story needs a few notes. Samuel's father was a Levite (1 Chron. **6**.33 f.). Levites were distributed among the tribes (e.g. Deut. **12**.12), probably for teaching purposes, and Elkanah was an Ephraimite Levite (1). The tabernacle and ark had been placed in Shiloh, about nine miles north of Bethel (Josh. **18**.1). By this time a solid structure had been built to contain them (1 Sam. **3**.3, 15).

Hannah might well have been tempted to relax her promise (11), but she made the sacrifice of parting with her child as soon as he could be left in the Temple (22–28). Being open towards God, she could pray and rejoice as she did (**2**.1–10).

*Compare* **2**.*1–10 with Mary's prayer of thanksgiving in Luke* **1**.*46–55.*

## 65 : The Open Way

### Psalm 27

In this third section of our studies we have already met men and women who were opened up to God in prayer—Abraham, Moses, and Hannah. They are all sinners, and yet in repentance, faith, and humility they have met God's forgiveness, and passed through to life in His presence, where prayer is natural.

The Psalms, forming the hymn book of the Bible, are as varied in their themes as any of our hymn books. This is a psalm of triumph, comparable to 'Praise, my soul, the King of heaven' (itself a paraphrase of Psa. **103**). We note the references to the open way. The Lord illuminates and saves; as I rest on Him, He gives confidence for life (1). In union with Him I am on His side in the battle against evil (2 f.). And yet it is not simply things and blessings that I want; it is the enjoyment of the Lord's presence and glory, and the joy of dependence on Him (4). The wording of v. 4 need not mean that a priest or Levite is the author, but it may be the prayer of a regular worshipper in the Temple, who also realizes, unlike so many in Israel, that the presence in the Temple is matched by the presence in the heart (7 f.).

He knows that God is concerned to bring him safely through periods of trouble, which indeed open the way again to the tent of the Supreme Commander and to the impregnable site where He stands (5). Again, the tent of inner security is reflected by the tent or Tabernacle (6), a title which describes the Temple because it was after the pattern of the wilderness Tabernacle and actually housed the old structure (1 Kings **8**.4), and also the term was a reminder that the Lord *camped* among them, and was not shut in a solid palace.

The psalmist is aware that, although he is in the tent of the King, he still has attachments on earth, and indeed his openness to God may close some human hearts against him. Enemies may make damaging attacks (11 f.). Even his family life may be threatened (10. Perhaps follow the NEB 'Though my father. . . .' or Jer. Bible 'If my father. . . .').

So when the way on earth is rough, there is still the open and level way to God (11 f.), and this is no escape from the land of the living, but the opening of the way for God to work in the events of life on earth (13 f.).

*Compare the thoughts of this psalm with Psa. **84** and Rom. **8**.31–39.*


# 66 : Companion by the Way

## Psalm 34

Although many scholars dismiss the descriptive titles of the psalms, and the NEB completely omits them, they may well give the original occasion of their composition, even if later David adapted them for use by congregations and individuals.

The incident of this title occurred in 1 Sam. **21**.10–15. It is difficult to estimate the rights and wrongs of David's actions during this period, but certainly he needed temporary escape from Saul's pursuit. As it was, he just escaped arrest by Achish and his men through pretending to be mad. But the break had made it possible for him to slip back into Saul's territory again. The title suggests that he wrote the psalm at Adullam (1 Sam. **22**.1). Its language not only describes recent deliverance, but contains pictures of refuge (8), sentries (7) and daily provisions (10), which were all vital at the cave of Adullam.

The psalm, however, goes far beyond David's temporary situation. He praises God for deliverance from Saul and Achish (4, 6), but wants to live in the constant openness of praise at all times (1–3). With a rueful allusion to his filthy face in the presence of Achish (1 Sam. **21**.13), he contrasts the radiance of the man who reflects God (5, cf. 2 Cor. **3**.18). In place of the scarcity of food, which he must often have suffered as he fled from place to place (e.g. 1 Sam. **21**.3 ff.), he finds in God the living bread (8–10, cf. John **6**.48–51).

The young warrior has already begun to learn the lesson of self-conquest, although his story shows that he still has much to learn. Here is one of several summaries in the psalms of the essentials of righteousness. The mouth reveals the heart (13, cf. Matt. **12**.34; Jas. **3**.2). Holiness is both negative and positive, and peace is to be our aim even if war appears inevitable (13 f.). God moves for the vindication of righteousness and the overthrow of evil (15–17). The righteous may be poor in spirit and afflicted (18, cf. Matt. 5.3–12), but the Lord is near them (18 f.).

In the light of the New Testament vs. 19–22 take on a fuller meaning. Complete deliverance may not come in this life, but the Lord brings us as whole people to be with Him (20, cf. 1 Thes. 5.23) at the Day of final redemption (22).

*Compare the thoughts of this psalm with Phil. 4.4–20.*

## 67 : Pilgrim's Progress
### Psalm 107

This psalm of suffering, insight, repentance and glorious restoration may well be compared with what we have read of Solomon's prayer in 1 Kings 8. It may have been sung when worshippers from all lands (3) came together at Jerusalem. They sing of God's ways in man's progress through life. The theme is the sad one that often people need to pass through personal tragedy to bring them back to fellowship with God and to praising Him from the heart in the repeated refrain of this psalm.

The first section (4–9) speaks of personal need rather than personal sin. The picture is literal, but is also true of the traveller on life's road, who finds himself in the wilderness of this world, like Christian in Pilgrim's Progress. He is concerned to make his way to the heavenly city (cf. Heb. 11.8–10, 13–16).

In the second section (10–16) we naturally pass again from the literal to the no less real inner experience. 'Every one who commits sin is a slave to sin' (John 8.34), and only the Son can break the bars of iron and set us free from the black dungeon (John 8.36).

Sickness (17–22) is part and parcel of the Fall, and, although the story of Job warns us not to say that every illness is punishment for personal sin, the Bible and psychology are clear that some illnesses certainly are. One may accept the original Hebrew text of *fools* (17, see margin) without changing the general interpretation of the section.

In vs. 23–32 the storm is not punishment for personal sin, but those who face terrifying natural forces are often drawn to cry for help to the great Creator. One cannot help drawing a parallel between the whole of this section and the story of the disciples in the storm (Matt. **8**.23–27).

The next section (33–38) somewhat resembles Hannah's thanksgiving (1 Sam. **2**.1–10) as it describes God's reversals for the wicked and the faithful. It may be illustrated by the descriptions of the state of Jerusalem in the Book of Lamentations, and by the restoration of prosperity after the return from exile.

The final verses (39–43) underline the lesson. Self-sufficient bosses collapse; those who are humble are raised up. We shall not see the completion of this process in this life, but meanwhile the average person still finds satisfaction in stories that vindicate the 'goodies' and punish the 'baddies' (42). Christians go further, and see that moral standards have their source in God (43).

*Consider how the physical experiences of this psalm may symbolize spiritual realities also.*


## Questions and themes for study and discussion on Studies 60–67

1. How did God help Abraham's faith by putting His promise into covenant form?
2. Make a list of occasions in the Bible when God's gracious choice of a person or group was quite different from what men might expect.
3. Do you think that the devotional atmosphere of the Psalter lends itself particularly to the revelation of God's compassion and mercy?
4. Do we learn more of the character of God from the way in which He describes it, e.g. to Moses, or from His actions? Could we manage with the one without the other? Consider this in the light of the New Testament also, e.g. the Cross and the New Testament interpretation of it.

# CHARACTER STUDIES

## 68 : Abimelech

### Judges 8.29—9.57

Gideon's strength gave peace to the land for forty years, but it was a peace which ended when his personal influence was removed by death. It was based too feebly on the influence of a personality, with no roots in God's law. After Joshua's death a tradition endured for a generation. Not so when Gideon went the way of all flesh.

The horrifying division of the land became again apparent. The town of Shechem, with its mixed population, was jealous of the hill hamlet of Ophrah. The old hankering for a king, after the fashion of the heathen world, arose, and on the wave of popular demand, Abimelech was swept to power.

Abimelech was a base and evil character. Financed by funds from a heathen temple, he staged a villainous *coup d'état*. Hiring a band of desperadoes, he waded to power through a river of blood. Gideon's work had begun with the throwing down of Baal's altar. Abimelech's career began with Baal's money used for mass murder.

It is a grim story. There is nothing to commend Abimelech. He is the living example of the successful adventurer, a man of Jehu's or Absalom's mould, but with none of Jehu's intellectual power, or Absalom's personal charm, a bleak, evil criminal. Jotham's keen wit was of no avail against him, uncanny though Shechem must have found the voice ringing from the top of Mount Gerizim, and telling the parable of the trees and their king. Jotham deserved better of his people than the exile which befell him.

94

Shechem had lifted Abimelech to power. Shechem betrayed him. Gaal, one of the inconsiderable characters in the story, led the revolt and won wounds and defeat. Apparent chance killed the villainous Abimelech, a death which, in his ludicrous pride, he thought shameful. A woman fractured his skull with a broken fragment of a millstone hurled adroitly from the tower-top. Abimelech, like the town which had first sponsored and financed him, reaped the crop of his sowing. To this internecine strife had God's people come. It was a Dark Age in the story of the land.

The sorry theme runs on to the end of the next chapter. Another period of over forty years is compassed with figures of faceless men flitting through the smoke, Tola and Jair of whom little is said. The raiders from the desert frontiers, the Phoenicians from the coast, press hard, and under the pressure the land cries for a leader.

## 69 : Jephthah

### Judges 11

A strange leader arose, a man of Gilead east of Jordan, a wild area of highland, the country of Jair, the last judge mentioned. Jephthah was no adventurer, thrusting himself, like the base Abimelech, into a vacant heritage. He was called to save his people from the pressure of the invaders, called from exile. It is not the only time in history that a rejected man has been summoned from the wilderness to lead his people. The list ranges from Moses and David to Churchill and De Gaulle.

Jephthah secured his guarantees, and began his leadership with an act of wise diplomacy. He gave Ammon a chance to withdraw, and in the approach he made demonstrated some knowledge of his nation's history. The tradition was not quite dead, in spite of the appalling ignorance which Jephthah was later to reveal. The Mosaic law was firm against human sacrifice. The consecration of the first-born had this for its aim and end. The story of Abraham and Isaac was designed to make clear, after the ancient dramatic fashion, that Jehovah was no Moloch, demanding a price of human blood.

Jephthah had no excuse for his foolish vow, and less for

carrying it to its horrible conclusion. He demonstrates the folly and the evil into which a man can fall when the truth is not patently before his eyes. Jephthah had faith. He is honoured by a minor place in the list of Hebrews 11.32, and yet his life was marred by a culpable ignorance of the character of God. What sort of demon did the rough judge imagine God to be, when he did his daughter to death in pursuance of a vow no man is called upon to make?

And yet men, unable to grasp the truth about the love of God and the completeness of salvation by faith, have more than once followed Jephthah's path. There have been periods in the history of the Church when the thought that God required appeasement by self-inflicted woe took hold of men like a darkness of the mind. The fourth century was soiled by the heresy. Jerome tells of a monk who for forty years drank nothing but muddy water. For six months Macarius of Alexandria slept in a swamp, and he always carried with him a load of iron. Bessarion never lay down to sleep. Most hideous of all was the asceticism of Simeon. He lived with a rope tied tightly round him, so that it cut into the festering flesh. He crept with vermin, and slept in a dry well. At last he found a pillar, one of the ruin remnants which strewed that falling world, and for thirty years, exposed to the rigours of all weathers, lived there incessantly bowing in prayer. Read Tennyson's poem: *Saint Simeon Stylites.*


## 70 : Jephthah's End

### Judges 12

Jephthah, for all the folly of his cruel sacrifice, must not be too harshly judged. His was a hard and shadowed youth, but he seems to have made an upright home, and it was tragedy indeed that he should mar it with self-made sorrow. For six years he lived with the memory of his murdered daughter, like Agamemnon of the Greek legend, clouded by his folly and his failure to understand the mind of God.

The civil war which was thrust upon him was none of his own making. The river proved a frontier of strife. The word 'rivus' is the Latin for a stream, and 'rivales' means those who share the same stream. That the word 'rival' should find such derivation has social significance. It is clearly part of history's experience that rivers form no divisive frontier like mountains and deserts, which keep hostile peoples apart. They cause dangerous confrontations. Hence 'the watch on the Rhine'.

Hence too, the clash between the tribes of Israel. Jephthah was a fighting-man, but he was no lover of war. As with the threatening people of Ammon, he did his best by diplomacy to turn Ephraim's jealousy aside. Ephraim was the head tribe of the house of Joseph. It occupied the heartland of Palestine, and lived in jealous suspicion of all eminence outside its borders. Ephraim challenged Gideon in his hour of triumph, and now they picked a quarrel with Jephthah. They looked upon the highlanders of trans-Jordan as a lesser breed to be taught their place. Jephthah is shown in a most honourable light. He did his best to avert strife. He reasoned and pleaded with his arrogant foes, and found no response. 'War,' said someone, 'is the continuation of diplomacy by other means,' and there is a grim measure of truth in the words. Jephthah was forced into the Jordan Valley civil war, and its subsequent horrors. Once in, he acquitted himself as Hamlet was bidden do:

> Of entrance to a quarrel, beware but, being in,
> Bear't that th' opposed may beware of thee.

Jephthah fought in sorrow. Sorrow had dogged his days from rejected youth to memory-ridden age. Age? Perhaps he died in his forties, worn out by all that life and his own folly had done to him.


## 71 : Samson's Parents

### Judges 13

More shadowy figures flit and pass. The tenth, eleventh and twelfth judges pass their undistinguished way. Few of them are clear-cut figures, as we peer through the darkness of that lamentable age in an endeavour to know them. With Samson comes a change. Perhaps a new chronicler has taken over in the Hebrew record. Perhaps the theme draws nearer to the days of some stability, when men remembered more fully, or had time for literature and the writing of history.

We know all we need to know: how thin and deviant had become the stream of historical purpose which flowed through Israel, how tragically the truth and its practice could be lost, and how lamentably surrounding heathendom could press upon the land . . .

With Samson comes something new, a sharply drawn and complicated personality, a person like ourselves, and something more than a vague figure with a sword or torch, some fierce-faced and alien man half glimpsed through the murk of a Dark Age. The story enters recognizable territory.

As though to prepare the way there comes a glimpse of Samson's parents. Manoah and his wife lived their lives of peasant peace in the horrible years the story has described. The Book of Ruth has a like story to tell of pockets of tranquillity among the sheltered hills, while the borders were aflame with strife. The childless couple, like 'God's poor' in Isaiah, like Amos, like Joseph and Mary, and a hundred others in Scripture, show that, for all the sin, backsliding and apostasy in high places, God had always what was to be called His Remnant, His Faithful Few.

Manoah and his wife are humble and pious folk, eager to know how best to rear the child so strangely promised to them. The child was to bring them sorrow. He was to fall far short of what he might have been, but he could never, through all the turbulence of his days, accuse the simple folk who had sought so anxiously to order his childhood, of having failed in their duty towards him. They sought to teach him self-control.

Poor Manoah! He appears once more, perhaps a score of years later (**14**.3), with a word of sane and scorned advice, and he died before the tragic end of the son who might have been so great (**16**.31).


## 72 : Young Samson

### Judges 14

A new enemy was on the borders. Down in what today is called the Gaza Strip, the Philistines had held a foothold and a colony since the days of Isaac, whose herdsmen clashed with theirs over water-rights. The Philistines were Europeans, a group of tribal expatriates from Crete, where what historians call the Minoan civilization had flourished for a full millennium. Originally, the group which gave Palestine (derived from Philistine) its name, may have been a trading-post. But Crete had fallen on evil days. Natural disaster and assault from the mainland, as far as it is possible from the findings of archaeology to fit the story together, had all but devastated the long island. At this time, in the twelfth century before Christ, and on into the days of Saul and David, there must have been a vast influx of people, with consequent search for living-space, and clashes with the occupiers of the hinterland.

It was a second invasion of the land. The Hebrew nomads had thrust in through the hill-country from the eastern wilderness. The Philistines drove in from the west and the Mediterranean. A clash, where the hills met the coastal plain, was inevitable. It was the first confrontation between Europe and Asia in history. And the Europeans brought culture, the art which may still be seen in the Palace of Knossos and other places in Crete, and their fish-god Dagon.

Perhaps this is what seduced Samson. It is possible to conjecture that the splendid young Hebrew, magnificently strong and keenly intellectual, might have been a missionary to Philistia. The one advantage the Hebrews had over the intruders from the West, was a clear and noble view of God. Perhaps the thirteenth judge might have been a conqueror of a different sort. Jephthah had dimly shown that there could be alternatives to war.

But Samson was a fool with women, and perhaps was fascinated by the culture of the foe. It is a recognizable situation. Among the Philistines he had popularity. Their bull-fighting, evident from the Cretan frescoes, shows evidence of their admiration for physical prowess. In this they were the forerunners of the Greeks. Samson was popular, and long tolerated in spite of the mischievous acts of vandalism in which he misused his strength.

Manoah was right. Samson had no right to marry outside the tribe. The chronicler's remark at (14.4) need mean no more than that out of Samson's folly God derived some military advantage for Israel. But surely God's first plan could rather have been that the fine young man should be a Jonah, an

Amos, a prophet messenger who might have brought blessing rather than blood.

## 73 : Samson's Folly

### Judges 15

Young men should read the story of Samson well. Bemused by the polished Philistines, despising the simple, chaste girls of the village community, where he had been born and taught, the young man Samson found a mate among the sophisticated young women of the alien. Curiously enough we know what the Philistine women were like from the frescoes of Crete. If they carried their national dress to Palestine, the women wore bustles and full-flounced skirts, contrasting with the bare-breasted cut of the bust. A greater contrast in appearance with the girls of the Hebrews could not well be imagined.

Milton's poem *Samson Agonistes* interprets the situation well. Samson had a first-class mind, as well as a magnificent body. He was of giant strength and superb daring, both qualities which women admire. He was no doubt under heavy siege from them, and the legends of Crete, which sometimes contain, as legends do, shreds of historical truth, suggest that the Philistine women had no great regard for moral purity.

Samson, too, had made friends among the people of the plain. One of them took his wife (15.2), for his marriage was, as he might have expected it to be, based as it was on a betrayal of ideals, a failure. Popularity, as well as his natural carnality, was his undoing. 'Like a petty god I walked about, admired by all,' Milton makes him say. He ended by betrayal right and left. The Philistines sought him to destroy him, and his own folk turned him over to the foe. No man can serve two masters (11–13). Samson learned that lesson in a bitter way.

Godless women, unholy fellowship with evil, compromising friendships, ruined Samson. It was as Milton makes the fallen hero say, 'through mine own default'. He betrayed his people, for it was a private war he fought with the Philistines, no crusade of national deliverance. He betrayed his God, for it was a dim faith and a travesty of Manoah's which he bore.

The true values which might have enriched his life were found among the rough tribesmen, not among the cultured pagans. True joy, true pleasure, true renown, lay with his own folk. He wasted his life in riotous living, the Prodigal Son of the Old Testament, undisciplined, capricious, carnal, violent for violence' sake. But Samson was the prodigal who came home dead.

## 74 : Samson's Failure

### 2 Corinthians 6

We should pause at this point to review the eternal laws which explain Samson's failure. William Neil in his small commentary remarks inexplicably that 'there is no obvious religious or moral value in the Samson stories'. Surely the moral lessons crowd every sentence.

Samson's usefulness depended upon 'separation'. Separation is a real principle of spiritual victory. God, and Samson's parents working under divine command, had brought him up as a Nazirite. This was a special calling, under two orders. There were temporary Nazirites, and permanent ones. Only Samson, Samuel and John the Baptist belonged to the latter class (Num. 6.1–21). The Nazirite calling was to fortify the future judge against the fierce temptations which Philistia offered.

This is why the suggestion has been made that Samson's real calling was to take God to the heathen plainsmen. He was trained to go among them, 'unspotted by the world'. He could help the Philistines only if he was separate from them. Hence the prohibition against alcohol. The Philistines, if inference may be drawn from the beer mugs discovered among the remains, were prodigious drinkers.

Samson kept the long hair, which was the symbol of his separation, but he forgot the reality, for surely Delilah could hardly have cut his precious locks had he not been lying in her room in a drunken sleep. It was 'gracious living', to be sure, down in Gath, the social drink, the free flirtation, cheap sexuality, and in the midst of it all, in Milton's powerful words, 'God disglorified, blasphemed, and had in scorn'.

Selfish and uncontrolled passion, forgetfulness of sacred

vows, led successively to loss of hair, the mere symbol, of power, the reality, of eyes and freedom. How many seek 'freedom' in a 'permissive society' and find bondage! The lessons which the commentator we have quoted failed to see? Simply these: Let youth commit to God the strength of mind and body, find a life-companion among God's people, learn early that love is God's gift and not to be soiled, keep separate from that which spoils, and stay in 'the Father's house'.

Let us close this note with Phillips' rendering of Rom. 13.12–14: 'The night is nearly over, the day has almost dawned. Let us therefore fling away the things that men do in the dark, let us arm ourselves for the fight of the day! Let us live cleanly, as in the daylight, not in the "delights" of getting drunk or playing with sex, nor yet in quarrelling or jealousies. Let us be Christ's men from head to foot, and give no chances to the flesh to have its fling.'

## 75 : Delilah

### Judges 16.1–22

Delilah, Samson's second wife, 'that specious Monster my accomplished Snare', as Milton makes him call her, was one of the bad women of Scripture. Curiously enough, Samson could see her baseness. He allowed her to deceive him, not once, but more than once. Milton again, in his tragic inter-pretation of the sad story, catches the situation aright. The foolish man, trapped by his carnality, walked the same path of folly again and again—

> *each time perceiving*
> *How openly, and with what impudence*
> *She purposed to betray me, and (which was worse*
> *Than undissembl'd hate) with what contempt*
> *She sought to make me Traitor to myself.*

He goes on, in Milton's poem, to tell how the evil woman battered the weary man—

> *Who with a grain of manhood well resolv'd*
> *Might easily have shook off all her snares.*

102

The poet touches well a point of psychological truth. Continual surrender to carnal sin produces a paralysis of resolution. The sinner, again, to quote Milton's perceptive poem, becomes 'the dungeon of himself'.

There is always 'a way of escape' (1 Cor. **10**.13) but it demands an act of will on the part of the tempted to rise and 'shake off the snares'. Bunyan had a word about Samson: 'Temptations, when we meet them at first,' he said, 'are as the lion which roared upon Samson. But if we overcome them, the next time we see them we shall find a nest of honey within them.' How very true—but the Hebrew Hercules, who could tear a lion apart, was a weakling in the hands of a woman whom he knew to be a liar and an agent of his enemies.

Delilah has had a numberless posterity. Bruyère, that keen observer of human character, followed by Tennyson, remarked that women can be better than the best of men—and worse than the worst. It would be difficult to find a baser character than Delilah, wheedling, feline, treacherous . . . But what can be expected of one who uses love for evil ends?

Milton makes Delilah come pleading for pardon. The text of Scripture gives no hint of this. Samson will have none of her. He rejects her touch—

> *At distance I forgive thee, go with that;*
> *Beware thy falsehood, and the pious works*
> *It hath brought forth to make thee memorable*
> *Among illustrious women, faithful wives :*
> *Cherish thy hastened widowhood with the gold*
> *Of matrimonial treason : so farewell.*

Delilah, serpent to the last, turns on the blind, doomed man and rejoices in her deed.

## 76 : Samson's End

### Judges 16.23–31

'Eyeless in Gaza, at the mill with slaves', Samson had time to think of what had befallen him:

> *. . . restless thoughts, that like a deadly swarm*
> *Of hornets arm'd, no sooner found alone,*
> *Rush upon me thronging, and present*
> *Times past, what once I was, and what am now . . .*

There can be no greater agony than the thought of irrevocable ill, the contrast past all remedy, between what might have been, and what turned out to be. Oscar Wilde's last poems, published after his early death in 1903, were contained in a volume significantly titled: *Hélas (Alas)*. These lines occur—

> *Surely there was a time I might have trod*
> *The sunlit heights, and from life's dissonance,*
> *Struck one clear chord to reach the ears of God.*

This might also have been true of Samson, the blinded slave who might have led a nation. He did nothing for Israel save massacre thousands of Philistines. And the Philistine menace remained—and worsened. Dagon was no rival, only a fish-god, born of the sick imagination of the maritime Cretans. Samson might have made peace by bringing Jehovah to the foe.

The end was service curtailed, and horrible death. House foundations in the area have revealed a pattern of building where the structure of a house rested on two adjacent pillars on a flat stone pediment. Samson sat between, and circled each pillar with an arm. Those who happened to look saw the ripple of mighty muscles in his back. They saw the great sinews of his arms start. They saw the crisped and blood-drained hands. They saw him give a fearsome lift, and 'bow himself' forward as he slid the two pillars, on which the structure of the roof depended, from their footing on the pediment on which he sat. In mighty ruin the roof caved in, and the walls fell outward. The crowded street without received the debris. In the packed eastern town adjacent structures were torn down with the falling ruin. It was sanguinary disaster. So Samson, the great 'might have been,' died. That God answered his last prayer does not prove its harmony with His highest purpose (cf. Psa. **106**.15). Dr Watson, the Victorian commentator, wrote: 'Not Milton's apology for Samson, not the authority of all who have likened Samson's sacrifice to Christ's, can keep us from deciding that this was a case of vengeance and self-murder, not of noble devotion.' If there was self-sacrifice in Samson, it was the sacrifice of a higher self to a lower. He destroyed Philistines—and deepened their hatred for Israel.

### Questions and themes for study and discussion on Studies 68–76

1. What New Testament illustrations can you quote for the fact that God appears to meet man on the level of his available faith?
2. What constitutes a 'call' to God's service? In what sense can a 'call' be a special one?
3. How did tradition and Moses' law make it clear that no human sacrifice was right?
4. The sources of temptation in a social context, and a secular culture.
5. What evidence of mental quality do you find in Samson's story?
6. In what ways can Samson's mistake of confusing symbol with reality be repeated in a modern setting?

# THE CHARACTER OF GOD

## A Merciful and Compassionate God
## (b) Proclaimed in Prophecy

### 77 : Announcement of the Gospel

**Isaiah 55**

This chapter should be studied as one of a sequence. Chapter **53** is the amazing death of the Lord Jesus Christ for our sins. Chapter **54** describes the new Israel that comes into being as a result, comprising Jews and Gentiles (**54**.1, cf. Gal. **4**.27). Chapter **55** then sets out the gospel appeal to individuals. Chapter **56** again speaks of the inclusion of all peoples (6–8). Thus in these chapters we see the Old Testament anticipation of the widening of Israel, even though the full revelation of entire equality of Jew and Gentile in Christ had yet to come (Eph. **3**.4–6).

Gospel preachers often quote **55**.1 f. as the free invitation to come just as we are. Isaiah links this to the work of Christ in vs. 3 f., as Paul points out in Acts **13**.34, which is a paraphrase of v. 3. The connection is the promise to David and to his descendants. Although David's descendants all failed to a greater or less extent, the prophets are shown that the final King, the Messiah, must be of David's line (e.g. Isa. **9**.7; **11**.1; Jer. **23**.5 f.). Since He has no successor, He must either be undying or be raised from the dead. In Isa. **53**.9 f. we see that He prolongs His life after death, and thus Paul is justified in linking **55**.3 with other verses that speak of His resur-

106

rection (cf. Heb. 13.20). The new covenant will be everlasting in a fresh sense, in that it is bound up in the ever-living Leader and Commander (4). And this new covenant will draw in others besides natural Jews (5, Eph. 2.12).

Now the Gospel appeal has the note of urgency (6), as previously it had the note of meeting deep need (1 f.). Now also comes the call to repentance (7), realizing that our ways are far below God's standards (8), and His way of salvation and ability to save are far beyond what man could possibly discover for himself (9, cf. 1 Cor. 1.18–25).

The Word of God is charged with power (10 f.), and it is possible to say that we are saved by the written and living Scriptures, inasmuch as we take the promises of God as they are there given, and the Word brings us to life and assurance. It is as though a millionaire were to rephrase v. 11 as 'My cheque will not bounce: it shall accomplish that which I purpose' (cf. Jas. 1.18; 1 Pet. 1.23–25).

The final section (12 f.) must be seen against the background of this group of chapters (40–55), which describe deliverance from Babylon and the return to the land, but the descriptions go far beyond the literal sense, in so far as they centre in Christ, the Suffering Servant. Thus we are to understand them today as describing deliverance from the world of sin (cf. Babylon of Rev. 17, 18) into the transformed life in Christ.

*To what extent is this chapter gospel preaching?*


## 78 : God in the Darkness

### Lamentations 3

This is an acrostic chapter, with each letter of the Hebrew alphabet in turn occurring as the initial of the three lines of every verse; but it is full of deep feeling. Some years have passed since the destruction of Jerusalem in 587 B.C., and the speaker now looks for the fulfilment of promises of return and renewal (e.g. Jer. 33; Ezek. 36).

At first his eyes are on his own sufferings as from the hand of God (1–18). In vs. 19–33 he turns to God in direct appeal, and claims His steadfast love. He is ready to wait patiently for the promised deliverance, knowing that God is concerned to bring a sufferer back when he is ready for it.

So far he has said little about sin, but in vs. 34–36 he laments the sins of oppression and injustice of which his nation had often been guilty. He admits God's hand in the blessings and sufferings of history, the goods and the bads (37–39). He calls for self-examination, so that other sins also may come to light (40–42).

At this point he is again conscious of the cloud that seemed to hang between God and himself (43–45). Yet, if he is in desperate grief for the stricken nation, how much more must God grieve (46–51). When he touches bottom, there is none but God to help; so even in the dark he cries again to Him (52–55), and suddenly knows that God has heard (56 f.).

It is difficult to disentangle the assertion of what God will do with those who persecute, and what the writer asks Him to do (58–66). Although the Babylonians and others had been used of God to bring the Jews to their senses, Lamentations shows that they had evidently poured in the extra brutalities that no one should properly inflict (cf. Amos **1**; Zech. **1.15**). So while the writer does not pray for their destruction, he asserts that God will hold them guilty for what they are doing while they dominate the land.

*Note that the well-known consolation texts in vs. 19–33 come from someone who had every human reason for despair.*


## 79 : God the Good Shepherd

### Ezekiel 34

This is a Messianic chapter that is less well known. The theme is the replacement of the false shepherds, the bad rulers, who manipulated everything in their own interest at the expense of others (1–6). These rulers included religious leaders.

The Lord's answer is twofold. (i) He must break the influence of the bad rulers (7–10); this He did in the exile. (ii) He will intervene Himself as the Good Shepherd to bring together

His scattered flock, including those that, being crippled, might be thought worthless (11–16, cf. Isa. 40.11).

The picture changes slightly in vs. 17–19. The leaders are now the stronger cattle that shoulder the weak away from the good pasture and fresh water, and then, after satisfying themselves, foul the remainder. One is reminded of much in the world of entertainment and literature today. Once more the Lord intervenes as the Good Shepherd to spoil the schemes of the dominant sheep (20–22).

Now comes the reference to the Messiah (23 f.), whom we know as the Good Shepherd incarnate (cf. the wording of v. 15). It is quite in accordance with Hebrew usage that He should be called David, as the final King of David's line (cf. Hos. 3.5). The close parallel with Jer. 23.1–8 shows that this is the correct interpretation; the King is not David himself.

The promises in vs. 25–31 are both literal and figurative. God brought His people back to the land, and, although at first they had a hard struggle (cf. Ezra and Nehemiah), they came through to prosperity and subdued their enemies. But bad shepherds took over again, and rejected the Good Shepherd when He came. Although the people again lost their land, the promises here are in terms that became pictures of the new life in Christ, the King Messiah (e.g. John 7.37 f.; 15.1–7; Rom. 11.17–24; Gal. 5.22 f.).

*Consider the contrasts between the false shepherds and the True. See e.g. Isa. 56.11; Jer. 25.34; Zech. 10.2 f.; 11.4–17; 13.7; Psa. 23; John 10.1–7; 1 Pet. 5.2 ff.; Heb. 13.20.*

## 80 : Mercy for the Prophet

### Jonah 1, 2

The story of Jonah is a piece of history chosen to show the concern of God for others besides Israel, and the way in which God's people may show rather less concern. Jonah lived in the reign of Jeroboam II soon after 800 B.C. (2 Kings 14.25). Assyria, with its capital of Nineveh, had been a scourge in Palestine, but was temporarily quiescent. History and archaeology show its brutality, and Jonah, hearing it was under the judgement of God (**1**.2), determined to let it perish without the chance of repentance (3). To flee from the presence of the Lord (3) meant that he gave up the right to be a prophet, since a prophet 'stood before the Lord' (1 Kings **17**.1). We also may flee to avoid commitment with the gospel to the pagan world.

Yet God would use Jonah and no one else, and through the terror of circumstances brought him to confession and humility, and to the acknowledgement of the God of all the earth (8–10). The pagan sailors were more anxious to save him from the judgement of God than he was to save the Ninevites (13 f.), but in the end they obeyed the prophet and prayed to the prophet's God for pardon if they were wrong (14).

Much has been written about the miracle of the great fish which Christ spoke of as true (Matt. **12**.40 f. See e.g. The New Bible Commentary). There have been at least two cases of a sailor surviving after being swallowed by a whale, though not for more than a short time. Jonah's preservation was miraculous, but understandable.

His prayer in ch. **2** is almost an anthology of sentences from the Psalms. He did, as we might do, and sang verses of hymns that he had stored in his memory, and no doubt there were many more than the few he records here. Enclosed in the belly of the fish, with only drowning awaiting him outside, he sees the symbols of the sphere of the dead (2, 6) and the wrath of God (3, 5, 6). Once he fled from God's favour (**1**.3), but now God's favour has been withdrawn from him (4).

Humble prayer and faith bring confidence (7), and he declares the deliverance that only the God of heaven and earth can bring (8 f.). And deliverance comes (10).

*Look up some of the parallels between ch. **2** and the Psalms if you have a Bible with full marginal notes. What aspects of God's acts has Jonah chosen ?*


## 81 : God's Mercy for Nineveh

### Jonah 3, 4

God probably gives His servants second chances more often than we realize. Jonah did not miss the second call. Nineveh as a city was enormously extended after 700 B.C., but Jonah here probably refers to the whole administrative area of his day (3, cf. 'Greater London'). He started in Nineveh itself, where the Assyrian king was in residence in his palace (6), and walked through the various streets all day, calling out God's message of judgement (4). The results were astounding, and the fear of God brought genuine repentance from evil and violence (5–8). So the doom was averted, and this is described in human experiential terms as the repentance of God. (cf. 1 Sam. **15** notes in Study 16.)

In ch. **4** it is Jonah who has to repent. He makes it clear that his reason for refusal to go was that he wished to see brutal Nineveh destroyed, but knew that God was merciful (2). In Psalm **27**.2 f. we saw that we must be on the side of God in wanting to see evildoers fall. We must equally be on His side in longing to see sinners salvaged when to our mind they do not deserve it.

Jonah still had a secret hope that he would see the city destroyed (5). His mixed-up ideas needed to be sorted out by an object lesson (6–11). He sat under a quick-growing plant that opened out to protect him from the sun. Next morning a grub destroyed it, and the sun became unbearable. Jonah was sorry for himself, but rationalized his feeling as sorrow for the poor plant which he had done nothing to cultivate. Now he is told to put himself in God's place. God, the Creator and Preserver of mankind, is concerned for the preservation of His Nineveh plant when the pest of sin would destroy it. If Jonah had seen the grub in the plant, he would have dug it out for the sake of the plant and himself. So why not be glad when he has been used to dig the grub out of Nineveh, with its inhabitants who have never had Israel's privileges— not to mention the animals?

*If you had to add a further verse after **4**.11, what would it be ?*

### Questions and themes for study and discussion on Studies 77–81

1. How do these passages and those in Studies 60-67 illustrate God's forgiveness?
2. It is easy to write of God's mercy and compassion when

things go well. How do these passages speak of it in adversity?

3. How do any of these passages and those in Studies 60-67 foreshadow the gospel?

4. Where else besides in Jon. 4.11 do we read of God's care for animals?

# CHARACTER STUDIES

## 82 : Micah

### Judges 17

The closing chapters of Judges seem designed to show the chaos of religious and civil confusion, the breakdown of worship and inter-tribal strife into which the land fell during this veritable Dark Age. Part of the story centres in the Ephraimite Micah, a man of means and position, who lived in the central hill-country.

The influence of Shiloh, the religious centre of Palestine, if any one place could, in such a time, boast that name, was so feeble that Micah conceived the idea of a family temple, complete with graven images (observe the plural) and a son of the household consecrated as a priest to serve them. To such a depth had the worship of Jehovah and the great Mosaic Code descended.

It was a great opportunity in Micah's eyes when a wandering Levite came that way. The fact that there were such mendicant priests on the road in Palestine is itself indicative of the collapse of centralized worship and authority. The man from Bethlehem was a type common in the European Middle Ages, a charlatan prepared to turn his reputation for sanctity to personal comfort and advantage.

The Levites had no special inheritance in the land, and in the general disorganization of religion were under heavy temptation to earn a living by their wits. The tithes that should have supported them were unpaid, and lesser men found some rational form of self-justification in preying on the community, and in meeting any popular demand which opened the way to such monetary and carnal advantage. To this had the heritage of Moses and Aaron descended.

And so the man from Bethlehem, for a wage of silver, a ration of clothes, and assured lodging (10), became the 'spiritual father' of Micah, who thought his wealth could secure him a private priest, access to God, and all the worldly advantages which men through all time have found in the practice of a cult. They are not unknown today, inside and outside the fabric of the professing Church. There are odd birds nesting in the mustard tree.

Observe the pathos of the last verse. Poor Micah had a Levite of his own, and it followed that divine blessing would follow. For a cheap rate he had secured the best that religion could give. As an antidote to the thought read Rom. **12**.1, 2.


## 83 : Moses' Descendant

### Judges 18

The well-told story in this chapter is revealing. Dan had not secured its heritage, so sent out from the country of Zorah and Eshtaol, the old district of Samson, some spies to seek for living-space. The men made two discoveries. They found Micah's secluded estate, his private chapel, and the fraudulent priest. The base man actually bestowed his blessing on their predatory enterprise (6). The second discovery was an idyllic community in northern Palestine, a forgotten colony of Phoenician Sidon, where the land was fertile, and where crime was unknown (7). It was such a community as men have dreamed about but seldom achieved.

The five scoundrels came back to report to their tribesmen in Zorah and Eshtaol, and the Danites set out with arms and a wagon train to migrate north. Passing through Ephraim they remembered the farmstead of Micah and the Levite of Bethlehem, who was the private priest. Bethlehem, after all, is only a dozen miles from Zorah and Eshtaol, and many of them knew the man. They decided to appropriate him along with the cultic images in the temple, which Micah had built and maintained.

Micah protested, but he and his farm labourers were no match for six hundred armed men of Dan. It suited the Levite to function as a tribal priest, rather than a household chaplain, so the column moved on, equipped now with their medicine-man. Micah had lost his religion, for religions thus built are easily taken away.

The Danites moved on into the peaceful Phoenician town, murdered its unsuspecting inhabitants, and settled on the appropriated land. They set up their graven image, and the heathen worship which went along with it. The Levite from Bethlehem became their permanent priest, and founded a sort of sacerdotal dynasty (30). But then comes the surprise. For the first time the calculating Levite from Bethlehem is named. He is Jonathan, son of Gershom, and Gershom was the son of Moses and Zipporah (Exod. 2.22; 18.3). If 1280 B.C. is accepted as the date of the Exodus, chronology just allows the possibility that Jonathan was Moses' grandson. But genealogies are seldom complete (e.g. the Lord, as 'the son of David') and two or three generations may lie between Gershom and Jonathan. But how tragic that a noble line should so decay.


## 84 : Naomi

### Ruth 1

The closing chapters of Judges are best passed over. They are recorded to reveal to those who read what can happen to a nation which forgets its God. They are history as Gibbon once described it: 'the register of the crimes, follies and misfortunes of mankind'.

The chronicler of the later chapters of Judges may easily have been a man of Bethlehem. That famous little town appears close to the events recorded. The Book of Ruth is also a tale of Bethlehem and probably comes from the same pen. It is vividly written and we sense the same capable hand which told the grim stories which close the major book. Ruth is also a tale of the Judges (1.1), and some instinct impelled the writer to make it a story apart.

That Elimelech should take his family across the Jordan and the Dead Sea into alien Moab, was perhaps the measure of his despair over the chaotic state of the land. The closing chapters of Judges give some indication of the evil which roved within a score of miles of his own home town. And there was always the menace of the raiding Philistines from the coastal lowlands.

It was, none the less, a tragic decision. Until quite recently a type of malaria was indigenous to the region, which fell with peculiar impact upon younger men. This may account for the deaths which widowed the gracious Naomi and took away her sons.

Perhaps Naomi's heart was never in the project. The history of more than one frontier has seen devoted women leave home and kindred with heavy hearts to follow an adventurous or restless family. Few have followed to tragedy more sad than that which fell to Naomi's lot. We have met citizens of Bethlehem in the story of the Judges, and they have not commanded admiration or respect. Naomi stands in contrast, and reveals that, in the most sombre times of a people's history, there can be godliness, sweetness and unselfishness among God's Few. Every word this woman utters is full of grace, thought for others, and godly simplicity. Naomi is the most womanly woman we have so far met since Eve—as Wordsworth put it:

> *A being breathing thoughtful breath,*
> *A traveller 'twixt life and death;*
> *The reason firm, the temperate will,*
> *Endurance, foresight, strength, and skill;*
> *A perfect woman, nobly planned*
> *To warn, to comfort and command,*
> *And yet a spirit still, and bright*
> *With something of angelic light.*

## 85 : Ruth

### Ruth 1.15—2.23

The quality of Naomi is revealed by the love and devotion she was able to excite. With words which have been made a part of the spirit of man, Ruth refuses to go back to Moab, to Chemosh (Moab's god) and the past (16 f.). She faces the future confident in another's love. There is a significant picture in her act of anyone facing the unknown, confident that Christ's care will be unwavering.

In all such decisions there is a counting of the cost and a cost to be paid. There are moments of doubt and of loneliness. Keats was no doubt right in his *Ode to the Nightingale,* when he pictured:

> *The sad heart of Ruth, when sick for home*
> *She stood in tears amid the alien corn.*

The young woman of Moab knew that she courted rejection among the Hebrews, who hated her race. She went with Naomi because she could not be happy apart from the mother she loved. To win such affection shows the worth of the one who won it. Naomi had her compensations.

Naomi returned to Bethlehem and, as so often happens, the old circle had closed. The place seemed different. She was hardly recognized, and the contrast between her present misfortune and her past felicity was made more painful and more keen by the sight of the familiar streets and the crowded houses on the ridge.

For Ruth, the whole environment must have been bitterly strange. There can be nothing more daunting than a foreign city where every word spoken reveals by turn of phrase and accent the gulf between the native and the stranger. Ruth met the situation with courage and hard work. Every instinct would suggest flight, and avoidance of confrontation. Instead, the young widow mastered herself and went out, as she was entitled by the Mosaic code of mercy to do, to glean in the harvest. The work was, no doubt, hard, and unrewarding. The Moabite was not welcome in the congregation of Israel, and it was only the marriage to a Hebrew, and the shield of Naomi's goodness, which covered her in her solitary task. Ruth had counted the cost and made her choice. And when choice of such sort has been made, it is well to abide by it. Ruth did, and won the reward of faithfulness.

## 86 : Boaz

**Ruth 3, 4**

We have met a gracious woman. We now meet a good and generous man. Those who read French will find a beautiful poem on Boaz by Victor Hugo, who, with fidelity to Scripture, pictures the old man of Bethlehem going out of his way in simple kindness to aid the weary girl who lingered in his field.

Naomi's directions, and Ruth's compliance involved no immodesty. It was the way of the East to communicate in symbols. The threshing-floor was an open space. The workers slept in their cloaks. It was thus that Boaz was made aware of his obligations as a kinsman—to marry the widow of the deceased relative, and continue his line. In the case of Ruth that line was to be an important one, as the list of her posterity, from David to Christ, reveals.

It is evident that, in the midst of wide forgetfulness of the Mosaic law, there was some memory of its social provisions, and the good Boaz had no hesitation in obeying as he was required to do, and meeting all the requirements of the law.

So the story moved to its happy ending, Boaz, Ruth and Naomi, all rescued from their varied loneliness and bereavement, and the brave, good woman, who had sought her home again after sad and distant wandering, rewarded by the holding of Ruth's child in her arms.

From the ridges where Bethlehem stands, far to the east, can be seen the purple edge of the mountains of Moab. The girl who had been faithful to a woman who had loved her could now look at the far line of blue with no home-sickness, but only joy for the discovery of a God who cared, guided and planned. The upward path from the floor of Jordan to the hills of Bethlehem had been hard upon the feet, but it was the path of love, decision and committal, and such paths lead home.

The book ends. We have met in its pages only love, goodness, faith, loyalty, kindness, obedience, generosity, mercy, fulfilment, courtesy—and never a deed or word of evil. And all these qualities and virtues have been shown only where they can be shown—in the persons of two women and a man.

**Questions and themes for study and discussion on Studies 82–86**

1. Discuss private interpretations of religion in the light of the authority of Scripture.
2. Collect from the Pentateuch the Law's provisions for foreigners.
3. Study the picture of the virtuous woman in Proverbs.
4. Collect from the Pentateuch the Law's requirements for the kinsman of a deceased person.
5. What historical principles may be derived from the narrative of the Judges?
6. What lessons arise from the story of Ruth?

# THE CHARACTER OF GOD

## A Merciful and Compassionate God
## (c) Exhibited in Christ

### 87 : Merciful as God

### Matthew 11.25—12.21

This section of mercy and compassion follows one of heavy judgement. Apparent wisdom can be completely misguided, and again and again God reveals Himself to those who look to Him in simple dependence (25 f., cf. 1 Cor. 1.18–21). The Son in His work goes the same way as His Father (27). In fact, these verses make sense only in the light of the revelation of the Trinity. Father and Son have that knowledge of each other that is possible only to those who are of the same Being (27, cf: John 1. 18; 1 Cor. 2.11). No mere man could honestly utter the astounding words of this verse.

Moreover, Jesus told men to come to Himself to find rest (28). A humble man, if mere man, would have pointed to God apart from himself. Yet Jesus Christ was in fact humble —the humble Servant bearing the Father's yoke and making it His own (29 f.). The word *gentle* (29) is the same Greek word as is translated *meek* in Matt. 5.5, and can carry the thought of an animal that is *trained*. This is a man's proper relationship to the Father, and Christ invites us to share it with Him. Unless we are truly one with Him, the yoke and burden may be irksome (30).

In 12.1–8 (cf. 1 Sam. 21.1–6) mercy in time of need takes

precedence over legality that would be unnatural. It was right to restrict the bread (Lev. **24**.9) and to observe the Sabbath, but not where sacrifice killed mercy (7, cf. Hos. **6**.6). There is the further hint of Christ's deity again here, since He takes precedence over the Temple (cf. 1 Kings **8**.27), and He is Lord of the Sabbath that God had consecrated (6, 8).

In vs. 9–14 Jesus again asserts mercy over a legality that would defeat its own reason for existence. A Sabbath that prevented healing was no Sabbath at all.

The quotation in vs. 18–21 of Isa. **42**.1–4 identifies Christ with the Servant who, as perfect Man, totally serves the Father. Man was made to be God-centred and not self-centred. Christ does not try for results by noisy demonstrations in the streets (19), even though He engaged in quiet and constructive preaching in the open-air. Moreover, He did not bulldoze His way through His hearers, but looked for the smallest signs of faith, as with the woman of Samaria (John **4**.7–30). We also should discern between those who need the strong rebuke of the so-called 'hot gospel' (**11**.20-24) and the spark which needs tender care to fan it to a flame.

*What examples are there of **12**.20 in the Gospels?*

## 88 : To be like God

### Luke 6.17–38

It is probable that this is not the same occasion as the Sermon on the Mount of Matt. **5**–7. Like any preacher with something worthwhile to say, the Lord repeated and adapted His teachings on several occasions. At the same time, sayings in the two sermons may well be compared, to throw further light on each.

Thus the poor of v. 20 may be those without money, but may also by analogy be the 'poor in spirit' of Matt. **5**.3. The kingdom is to be humbly received, not bought. The hunger of v. 21 may be literal, but it also symbolizes an appetite for God-likeness that only God Himself can satisfy (Matt. **5**.6). Weeping (21) or mourning (Matt. **5**.4) can take in grief for personal and world sin and need.

By contrast the rich are too easily satisfied with this world, and ignore the permanent kingdom of God (24). The full find material food is all they need, and leave the longing for God-likeness to others (25). The good-timers ignore the serious claims of life (25). The second group live for the standards of their good-time friends, as did the false prophets (26, e.g. Jer. **6**.14; Mic. **2**.11). The first group suffer with Christ (22 f.). Each is 'rewarded' on the basis of this life not being the ultimate aim for living.

Christ singles out some points of God-likeness for His followers. We must go out actively in love, even to our enemies (27 f.), and continue to treat them with non-natural generosity (29 f., cf. Matt. **5**.43–48). It is all very well to have a good spirit among friends (31–34), but a different matter to show the same spirit to those who dislike us (35). Yet we are to be generously kind like God our Father (36).

In vs. 37 f. we have what is almost a natural truth, in the sense that God has naturally made mankind so that the man who is generous in thought, word and deed drops the usual human barriers, and people are drawn to him in respect and trust. He gets what he gives. Similarly with God; 'Love so amazing, so divine, demands (shall have) my life, my soul, my all.'

*Compare any parallels between this section and the Sermon on the Mount.*


# 89 : God calls the Gentiles

## Acts 10

A key thought of this chapter is that God moves to bring an earnest Gentile seeker to Himself. The acceptability of which Peter speaks in v. 35 is not the salvation of Cornelius as he stands, for he still needs to hear and respond to the gospel (Acts **11**.14). But, faced with a genuine seeker, God calls His messenger to go to him.

Peter has been given the keys of the Kingdom by Christ (Matt. **16**.19), and he uses them to open the three doors— to the Jews at Pentecost (Acts **2**.14), to the Samaritans, who were semi-Jews in faith and race (**8**.14), and here to the Gentiles. While he was willing enough for the first two, his whole tradition made him recoil from full admission of Gentiles, and consequently he needed the special vision of the clean and unclean beasts.

Once he was convinced of the meaning of the vision, he went forward step by step in the path of God's plan, even though he could not as yet understand what it would be. Final doubts were swept away by God's act in pouring out a Gentile Pentecost before the converts had been accepted for baptism. There was so much prejudice against the admission of Gentiles that Peter later used this initiative from God to vindicate his action in receiving them (**11**.15–18; **15**.7 f.).

This chapter naturally raises speculation on the state of true seekers, who have the right to hear the gospel of redemption, but who, maybe because of our reluctance to go, fail to hear it. The Bible never gives a direct answer to this, probably because any promise of a second type of salvation-experience would encourage us to hang back even more from our evangelistic responsibilities. All we are told is that we must go to a world that is perishing. Some without the gospel are more ready than others, and Peter recognizes that this applies to every nation (35).

*Why would it have been inconsistent with God's character to refuse full membership of the Church to the Gentiles? Why was it consistent under the Old Covenant?*

## 90 : The Glory of being a Christian

### Ephesians 1

God is the God of all riches, which He has shared with us in Christ (3). 'In Christ' is a repeated key phrase of this letter to describe a deep, and not fictitious, union. 'The heavenly places' (3) occurs five times, and describes, not heaven itself where we shall be one day, but the sphere of union with Christ who is in heaven in the place of all authority.

God chose Israel freely (e.g. Deut. **7**.7 f.) to live out His holiness (e.g. Exod. **19**.5 f.), and He has similarly chosen us in Christ (4). Yet in Christ we are more than His people;

we are His children (5) with all that children need (6). His valuable gifts begin with redemption through the sacrificial death of His beloved Son (7 f.), and the whole amazing plan is being worked out to unite the whole universe under Christ (9 f.). The Jews were the first to share in the new salvation, since they had been prepared (11), but almost at once the door was opened for us Gentiles, who have been marked out by the Holy Spirit as those who belong to Christ and who will eventually have the full enjoyment of our inheritance (13 f.).

Now follows the first of two great prayers for the Ephesians, and ourselves, to enter practically into what is ours in Christ. After thanksgiving come requests; (i) For illuminated perception that knows God—not just facts (17). (ii) For a heart set on the wealth of eternal things, and on divine, rather than human, values. Conversely, we remember that we in our turn are amazingly God's inheritance (18). (iii) For the inner power that we need and that God gives beyond measure (19, cf. 3.20), for this is the same power as was seen in the resurrection, ascension and exaltation of the Lord Jesus Christ (20). He is the Lord of space and time, of the whole visible and invisible universe (21). Amazingly we share His rule, inasmuch as He is the head while we are the body, which is filled by His life as our physical bodies are filled with natural life. But His life which we share is more than a life that is confined to the Church. It is the life of the Creator and Sustainer of the universe (23, cf. Col. 1.17 f.).

*Compare this chapter with Col. 1.*

# 91 : The Way Into God

## Ephesians 2

From the glories of ch. 1 we come down to the struggles on earth. Once we were dead because our sinful state cut us off from the living God (1). Our way of thinking and behaving was that of the world, the flesh, and the devil (2 f.), so that we lived as though there was nothing beyond what can be experienced on earth, and therefore we took all that we could from the present. We were under the wrath of God, because God hates this way of living and thinking (3).

God's wrath is not departmentalized as ours often is. It merges into mercy and outgoing love (4). He did not wait for us to reform and somehow come to life, but spontaneously called us and made us alive in Christ (5). So salvation contains more than legal acquittal, which is the subject of Romans 4, 5. It also links us to the living and triumphant Christ (6); what He has begun God will also complete in Christ (7).

As in Romans, Paul emphasizes the focusing of grace and faith in our experience of salvation. We cannot tell how one blends with the other. All that we know is that we are not saved through our own good works (8 f.). In fact, we can see ourselves as God's good works, moving forward as new creations in Christ Jesus to be like Him (10).

Next comes the Gentile charter at a time when some Jewish Christians were still suspicious of Gentiles. Once they were outside the covenant of life that God made with the Jews (11 f.). Now the covenant is no longer national, but exists in Christ (13), so that to be in Christ is to be a full member of the new body. The cross, not the law, is the place of reconciliation for Jew and Gentile alike. Reconciled to God, they are reconciled to one another (14–16).

We note the significance of the Trinity (18) as we come to the Father as citizens, family, and living stones of the living temple (19–21). The order of building is first Christ, then the apostles and inspired teachers, and then the worldwide Church members. The temple was the focus of God's presence on earth. The Church on earth and in heaven similarly should be the temple that radiates God because He is its inner life (22).

*These words about the acceptance of the Gentiles seem beside the point now. Are they really? Is there room for everybody in our congregations today?*

## 92 : Full Members in Christ

### Ephesians 3

The Old Testament reveals that all nations (Gentiles) will come to share the blessings of Israel and the Jews. But nowhere is it revealed on what terms they would come in, and it was assumed that the Jews would be the superiors and that Gentiles would have to accept the Jewish Law.

Paul here declares that what was concealed from the Old Testament prophets has now been revealed by direct inspiration to the apostles and prophets of the Christian Church (5). This revelation is that the body of Christ has now become the recipient of the Old Testament promises, and consequently all members of the body lose their separate identity as Gentiles or Jews (6) and all inherit the promised mercies and riches of God.

Although Paul had been brought up as a strict Jew (Phil. 3.5 f.), he was chosen by God as the special interpreter of the gospel to the Gentiles (7 f., cf. Gal. 2.7–9). He preached Christ in all His richness rather than the temporary law (8), and showed that in Christ God was doing more than establishing a nation on earth; He was carrying the battle and the victory into the realm where unseen opponents still contest the rule of Christ (10, cf. 6.12). We are to go boldly by faith into the presence of God, knowing that there is a battle, but that in Christ we can conquer (11–13).

The prayer that follows takes us to the heights of heaven and to the inner shrines of the spirit. We notice again the place that is given to the Trinity; each Person has His function, but the presence of One is the presence of All. We approach the Father in heaven, who gives parent/child meaning to all family relationship on earth (14 f.). We ask for inner strengthening through the incoming of the Spirit (16), and through the faith-link with Christ (17), which is like the cord that joins the unborn baby to its mother. Faith does not create the indwelling; it accepts and acts upon it in love (17).

We must have the unlimited heavenly vision (18), and experience the paradox of knowing what we cannot know, the full love of Christ, being filled with God's inexhaustible life (19). We rightly say 'Impossible', but God's inner power is beyond all imagination (20). To Him be the glory! (21).

*Compare some Old Testament prophecies about the Gentiles with what Paul says here. E.g. Psa. 96; Isa. 45.22 f.; Mic. 7.16 f.; Zech. 8.22 f. How far is there a further step in God's reception of all mankind in the Christian Church?*

# 93 : God is Totally Love

## 1 John 4.7–21

In this final portion the nature of God is summed up as love. It has been pointed out that v. 8 does not say that 'love is God'. The English word *love* comes under many forms, but this chapter shows how it reaches its height in divine fact and Christian experience. It is difficult not to kill it by analysis.

If love is the total summary of God's outgoing, no one can truly have God's nature born in him without showing this love in considerable measure (7 f.). God's love streamed into history when He sent His Son that we might have life through His death (9). This action came spontaneously from God and was not in response to our love (10). But if we accept His love for us, we are caught up into His practical love for others also (11). Although as yet we have not seen God face to face, we express our fellowship with Him by sharing His life of love (12, cf. 1 Cor. 13.12 f.).

Yet our testimony is not only to our experience of love, but to the concrete facts of the gospel which God has revealed (13). Who is Jesus Christ, and why did He die (14 f.)? How does this reveal the love of God, and how do we come to experience it (16)?. How can we have confidence in the day of judgement when we know how unlike God we still are (17)?

John is not teaching sinless perfection (cf. 1.8). It would seem that here faith and love come close together, as in Gal. 5.6. Faith which works by love casts out the fear of judgement (18) because we have the assurance of the finished work of Christ (19) and see the love of God working out in practical living (20). But this is not left to feeling; it is backed by a straight command (21, cf. Matt. 22.37–39; John 13.34 f.).

*Consider the meaning of 'Son of God' (15). Can it mean one who is less than God? If so, is the love of God less than it might have been, since He sent someone other than Himself?*

## Questions and themes for study and discussion on Studies 87–93

1. What criteria do these New Testament passages give for the Christian life as being grounded in God?

2. Who initiates salvation and why?
3. Compare the prayers in Eph. **1**.15–23; Eph. **3**.14–21; Phil. **1**.9–11; Col. **1**.9–12 as expressions of sharing in the richness of God.
4. If Christ totally exhibits the character of God, what does it mean to be 'in Christ'?